Pennie Foster-Fishman

Contents

Foreword ·· （Ⅶ）

Contributors ·· （Ⅹ）

Acknowledgements ··· （Ⅻ）

1. **Learning by doing in Guizhou and Yunnan provinces** ············· （1）
   Opening a new window on research practice ························ （3）
   The interest in a PM&E process ······································ （4）
   The approach and process ··· （5）
   Key elements in capacity-building for PM&E ····················· （7）
   The project teams ·· （9）

2. **Building a common understanding: core concepts and methods**
   ·· （22）
   Defining participatory, monitoring, and evaluation ··············· （23）
   The magic wheel of PM&E ·· （28）
   Why? — defining the goals ·· （31）
   For whom? — identifying the users ································· （33）
   What? — defining the object ·· （34）
   Who? — identifying the implementers ····························· （42）
   When? — establishing the timing ·································· （45）
   How? — selecting the tools ·· （46）
   Synthesis ··· （48）

3. **"We help them, they help us": experience in Yunnan** ············· （55）
   PARDYP: goals and process ·· （55）

The participants ·· (57)

Work in the field: activities and outcomes ···························· (58)

    Participatory project planning ··························· (59)

    Monitoring and evaluation of activities ················· (67)

    Feedback meetings ···································· (74)

    Planning new activities ································ (85)

    Second round of meetings to plan the new activities and further

    monitoring ··· (87)

Reflections ··· (93)

4. **"Now we manage our water well": monitoring natural resource use in Guizhou** ·· (96)

Outcome of the first PM&E training workshop ······················ (96)

Draft plan for fieldwork ·· (97)

The first round of fieldwork ······································ (98)

Feedback and adjustments ·· (108)

What we learned at the second PM&E training workshop ············ (110)

The second round of fieldwork ···································· (111)

Issues emerging from the fieldwork ································ (120)

Lessons learned ··· (121)

Conclusions ·· (122)

5. **"Realizing our dreams": participatory project evaluation in Guizhou**
·· (124)

Assessment of village performance ································ (124)

Participatory evaluation of the GAAS project at the community level
·· (128)

Project evaluation in non-participating communities ················ (137)

Reflection at the project team level ······························· (141)

Project evaluation at the government level ························· (144)

Synthesis ·· (146)

6. **Making room for change: progress and challenges** ·············· (148)

The value of PM&E ·· (148)

A balancing act: the training method and process ················· (150)

Future steps ··· (153)

Appendix 1. Programs for the three workshops ············· (155)

Appendix 2. Exercises carried out at the three training workshops

··· (159)

References ·· (169)

About the editors ···································· (173)

Figures

Figure 1. Sketch map of location of Yunnan and Guizhou in southwest China (above) and Project sites (below) .... (2)

Figure 2. The PARDYP project cycle .... (17)

Figure 3. The magic wheel of PM&E .... (29)

Figure 4. Stages in the PM&E action plan at the project level .... (30)

Figure 5. Stages in the PM&E action plan at the program level .... (30)

Figure 6. The PARDYP PM&E process from July 1999 to June 2001 .... (56)

Figure 7. Map of the Xizhuang watershed .... (59)

Tables

Table 1. Comparison of conventional monitoring and evaluation and PM&E
.... (24)

Table 2. Results of exercises carried out by the GAAS project team at the
first workshop .... (50)

Table 3. Results of exercises carried out by the KIB project team at the
first workshop .... (51)

Table 4. Results of matrix scoring and ranking of livestock with four
households in Damaidi village .... (64)

Table 5. Local criteria for ranking wealth in Yangjia .... (65)

Table 6. Results of matrix scoring and ranking of fruit trees with six
farmers from different households in Yangjia .... (66)

Table 7. Example of an information chart prepared by farmers during the
project planning phase .... (69)

Table 8. Economic comparison of crops grown in Yangjia .... (72)

Table 9. Benefits of nine small projects in Damaidi, identified by groups
of villagers .... (81)

Table 10. Multi-stakeholder framework for PM&E of water management
system (GAAS project team) .... (100)

Table 11. Action plan for the fieldwork of the GAAS project team ... (101)

Table 12. Ranking of problems in the water management system in
Dabuyang and perceived reasons for them .... (103)

Table 13. Ranking of problems in the water management system in
Dongkou and perceived reasons for them .... (107)

Table 14. Characteristics of the four villages involved in the second
round of PM&E fieldwork .... (111)

Table 15. Locally defined indicators of economic status of households
at the GAAS project site (1998) .... (112)

Table 16. Summary of comments recorded in self-monitoring booklets
by 10 households in Dabuyang (2000) ·················· (113)

Table 17. Summary of comments recorded in self-monitoring booklets
by 6 households in Xiaozhai (2000) ·················· (116)

Table 18. Summary of comments recorded in self-monitoring booklets
by 10 households in Dongkou (2000) ·················· (118)

Table 19. Summary of comments recorded in self-monitoring booklets
by 10 households in Chaoshan (2000) ·················· (119)

Table 20. Villagers' indicators of effective and efficient water management
(GAAS project) ······························· (120)

Table 21. Assessment of village performance based on farmer-established
criteria (average scores) ······················· (128)

Table 22. Participatory project evaluation meetings — when, where,
and who ··· (129)

Table 23. The most effective project interventions, by village ········· (133)

Table 24. The least successful intervention, by village ··············· (136)

Table 25. Experiences to share with others ·························· (136)

Table 26. Sources of information about the GAAS project listed by
villagers from Napeng and Chaobai ·················· (138)

Table 27. GAAS project interventions that were best known to farmers
in Napeng and Chaobai ·························· (140)

Table 28. GAAS project activities that Napeng and Chaobai villagers
wanted to learn about most ······················· (141)

Foreword

This volume presents a remarkably compelling and frank account of the most recent of a series of actions undertaken over the last decade by scientists in southwest China to integrate the concerns and work of rural men and women into applied research and development to alleviate poverty. These chapters describe and assess the first efforts in China to incorporate participatory monitoring and evaluation into actual project cycles. The "learning by doing" training approach brought about a partnership between researchers, project area farmers, extensionists, and local government officials to systematically monitor and assess the relevance and performance of project work. This strengthened farmer participation in the work and, in Guizhou, led to the introduction of self-monitoring mechanisms for the management of local water resources by farmers. These efforts also deepened the understanding of researchers and local officials of how the various interests and concerns of poor rural men and women are represented and negotiated in research and development work. Not only what is assessed matters, but also who does the assessment. This, in turn, has strengthened the learning, accountability, and effectiveness of the teams' efforts.

By the late 1980s, a new generation of southwest Chinese scientists had come of age professionally. However, they were increasingly frustrated by the enormous gulf that lay between official accounts of rural conditions and progress in reform-era China and real life in multi-ethnic mountain communities in Yunnan and Guizhou. At provincial levels, most government analyses of rural poverty and development relied, at best, on idiosyncratic interviews of county-level officials, the tired and problematic standby of traditional Chinese statecraft — "seeing flowers from horseback." Most agricultural station research was solely production oriented, often without regard to even basic concerns about socioeconomic or environmental appropriateness to lowland Han farmers in central China, much less to the complex, multitiered, and multi-ethnic mountain ecologies and social systems of the headlands of the great rivers of

Asia.

Despite the profusion of rosy accounts of reform and potentials, even cursory visits to uplands rural communities in the southwest revealed appalling poverty, largely untouched by decades of state programs. Aggregate statistics also showed an alarming stagnation in rural productivity growth and incomes and declines in rural terms of trade. These trends persisted through the mid-1980s and 1990s, once the early gains resulting from devolution of some decision-making to farm households, more widespread marketization, availability of modern farm inputs, and price liberalization were exhausted.

The young scholars also faced a difficult institutional context. Most of the tools of rural sociology or cultural anthropology were largely unknown and officially suspect. The few policy-advisory and decision-making positions in provincial government agencies, which were traditionally reserved for promising young researchers, had just been filled by the first cohort of post-Cultural Revolution college graduates. At the same time, the still relatively underdeveloped private sector kept many of the best of this highly committed second cohort in research. Province-based scientific research institutions had extremely limited capacity for research and were chronically underfunded. Still-strong commandist-era sectoral hierarchies inhibited collaboration between and across institutions. Governance problems, subsumed for much of the reform period by the rapid pace of economic reforms, were increasingly central.

However, their very remoteness from centres of power and the weakness of provincial government resources allowed greater scope for experimentation with new partners and approaches. New materials were available to these researchers, describing ever more widespread work outside China on participatory development approaches. By the late 1980s, a few international development agencies and NGOs were permitted to begin work in rural areas of these poorest Chinese provinces.

Through this last decade, a small number of rural researchers in Yunnan and Guizhou persisted in efforts to narrow the gulf between the rhetoric of province-level development programs and analyses and the reality of life in poor upland communities. Early rapid rural appraisal efforts compelled longer-term and increasingly participatory studies of rural land use and tenure, resource dynamics, health care, technology development, and gender and social heterogeneity. These, in turn, led to efforts to share emerging learning and approaches through training and mentoring in more extensive and younger networks of provincial researchers and subprovincial government officials — across institutions and expanding urban civil society — through the establishment of participatory rural appraisal networks in Yunnan and Guizhou.

Two groups around which this work centred are the Kunming Institute of Botany of the Chinese Academy of Sciences and the Guizhou Academy of Agricultural Sciences. In their most recent research and development plans, these organizations proposed to our International Development Research Centre the introduction of continuous participatory monitoring and evaluation activities to strengthen their unstinting rural research and development activities. In describing and reflecting on this training approach, this volume fills an important gap in assessing its value in real world settings. We are proud to have supported this important work and trust that it finds a broad audience among practitioners and theorists in China and elsewhere who are interested in participatory research and development.

Stephen J. McGurk, Regional Director
Office for Southeast and East Asia
International Development Research Centre

Contributors

Guizhou Academy of Agricultural Sciences, Guiyang, Guizhou

Integrated Rural Development Centre

Chen Deshou, senior researcher, bachelor's degree in agronomy

Li Yourong, researcher, master's candidate in environmental studies

Li Zhinan, researcher, master's candidate in sustainable development

Pan Jiawen, senior researcher, bachelor's degree in agronomy

Yin Dixin, senior researcher, bachelor's degree in agronomy

Yuan Juanwen, researcher, master's degree in social forestry

Zhao Zeying, researcher, master's candidate in management science

Zhou Pidong, senior researcher, master's degree in development
    management/agronomy

Soil and Fertilizer Institute

Xia Yuan, researcher, master's degree in development management

Kunming Institute of Botany, Department of Ethnobotany, Chinese Academy of Sciences, Kunming, Yunnan

Fan Lizhang, researcher, master's degree in meteorology

Gao Fu, researcher, master's degree in ethnobotany

Mas, Stephanie, researcher, master's degree in development studies

Qian Jie, researcher, master's candidate in social development

Sha Liqing, researcher, master's degree in soil sciences

Wang Jianhua, researcher, master's degree in ethnobotany

Wang Yuhua, researcher, doctorate in ethnobotany

Yang Lixin, researcher, bachelor's degree in forestry

Yang Yongping, associate professor, doctoral candidate in ethnobotany

Yang Xuefei, researcher, master's degree in ethnobotany

Yang Zhiwei, researcher, bachelor's degree in agronomy

Baoshan Hydrology Bureau, Baoshan, Yunnan

Ma Xing, associate engineer, bachelor's degree in hydrology

Baoshan Forestry Bureau, Baoshan, Yunnan

Zhao Mingshou, forestry technician, college degree in forestry

Centre for Biodiversity and Indigenous Knowledge, Kunming, Yunnan

Zhang Lanying, head Capacity Building Division, master's degree in development management/Filipino linguistics (before joining CBIK, Ms. Zhang Lanying was the China program coordinator of the International Institute of Rural Reconstruction)

Acknowledgements

Early in 1999, an idea was born; two Chinese research teams would be brought together in a training process to strengthen their monitoring and evaluation skills. A few months later, the teams — one from Yunnan, the other from Guizhou — met for the first time and began their journey of learning.

It proved to be a joyful and interesting, but also demanding voyage. Joyful, because we made new friends and had good times together. Interesting, because we learned a lot from sharing experiences, insights, and ideas with each other. Demanding, because reflecting on our own work made us (more) aware of shortcomings, gaps, and opportunities for improvement.

We would like to thank our supporters and guides who encouraged us to continue on our chosen path. Our research teams and colleagues at the Kunming Institute of Botany and the Guizhou Academy of Agricultural Sciences enthusiastically embarked with us and remained on board (sometimes wondering where we were all going).

Without the support provided by the women, men, and children at the local level (in the villages, townships, and counties), we would have been lost from the very beginning. We warmly thank the farmers and government officials living and working in the Xizhuang watershed (Yunnan) and Kaizuo township (Guizhou) for their enthusiasm and patience, the knowledge they shared with us, their ideas and visions, and their tolerance of the mistakes we made.

All along the way, we received encouragement from colleagues in the Community-Based Natural Resource Management program at the International Development Research Centre and at the Ford Foundation. We extend a *xie xie* to John Graham, Stephen Tyler, Liz Fajber, Brian Davy, Guy Bessette, Claire Thompson, Brenda Lalonde, Marleny Tanaka, Elaine Tang, Stephen McGurk, Gary Newkirk, Hans Schreier, and Hein Mallee. Ms. Fong Ku was an invaluable tracker at the very beginning of our journey.

This book is a team effort. The various chapters build on workshop and fieldwork reports and other papers produced by the teams over the course of the training project. However, certain authors took the lead on individual chapters and we want to recognize this role. Ronnie Vernooy is the lead author for chapters 1 and 2 — the introduction and the description of the key concepts. Stephanie Mas and Qian Jie of the Kunming Institute of Botany put together chapter 3, describing the PM&E experience in the PARDYP project. Zhou Pidong, Sun Qiu, Li Zhinan and Yuan Juanwen of the Guizhou Academy of Agricultural Sciences (GAAS) are the lead authors for chapter 4 on the PM&E experience, with emphasis on project *monitoring*, in the GAAS project. Sun Qiu (GAAS), Zhang Lanying (CBIK) and Chen Deshou (GAAS) are the lead authors describing the project *evaluation* work in the GAAS project in chapter 5. All the contributors and the three editors joined hands in Chapter 6.

Our efforts to record this story (at the "end" of the road) received critical support from Sandra Garland, Bill Carman, and Mrs. Li Hong. They managed to make sense of our experiences and our, sometimes, chaotic thoughts.

Picture 1, The GAAS project site in Guizhou province

Picture 2, Farmers are tasting
different varieties of rice
in the GAAS project

Picture 3, Farmers are scoring different
varieties of rice using PRA tools
in the GAAS project

Picture 4, The PARDYP project site in Yunnan province

Picture 5, Focus group discussion with farmers about
PM&E indicators in the PARDYP project

Picture 6, Farmers are scoring different cash crops
using PRA tools in the PARDYP project

Picture 7, The coordinators of the GAAS and PARDYP projects exchange ideas during the 1ˢᵗ PM&E training workshop in 1999, Guiyang

Picture 8, GAAS and PARDYP team members join forces to do an evaluation exercise known as "the knot"; second PM&E training workshop in Kunming, 2000

Picture 9, Group work and learning during the 3ʳᵈ PM&E training workshop in 2001, Baoshan

Picture 10, The GAAS and PARDYP teams design a first PM&E plan during the 1st PM&E workshop

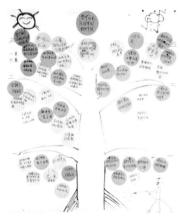

Picture 11, The tree diagram of lessons learnt and difficulties in the different stages of implementing PM&E; 3rd PM&E training workshop

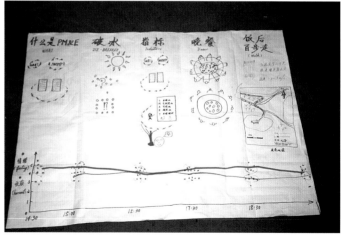

Picture 12, Participatory monitoring tool designed by the GAAS and PARDYP teams during the 1st PM&E training workshop to keep track of daily activities and results

1. Learning by doing in Guizhou and Yunnan provinces

We re-elected our village leader. The former leader was not strong-willed and not wanting to assume responsibility for sharing his time for the common good of the village. We employed a group responsibility system to manage forest and wastelands clarifying the rights, duties and benefits of group members. This strategy encouraged farmers to plant trees; last year, we planted more than 20 000 trees on the wasteland. The tree survival rate was as high as 94%. We also installed a drinking water system, but unfortunately the water source does not provide enough water. We are unable to make good use of the system. From this we learn that when we make a decision we have to be careful and consider the different aspects of things. — Niuanyun village resident, reflecting on progress made by the Community-Based Natural Resource Management project in Guizhou, in a monitoring meeting with researchers from the Guizhou Academy of Agricultural Sciences

This book is about the experience of two research teams in Yunnan and Guizhou provinces in southwest China (Fig. 1) who carried out a participatory monitoring and evaluation (PM&E) project. PM&E is a joint effort or a partnership between researchers and other stakeholders (such as farmers, government officials, or extension workers) to monitor and evaluate, systematically, one or more research or development activities (for a discussion of the core elements of PM&E, see Armonia and Campilan 1997, Abbot and Guijt 1998, McAllister and Vernooy 1999). Focusing on participatory field research in the area of community-based natural resource management, we aimed to contribute to the (still scarce) literature on PM&E, especially conceptual, methodological, and capacity-building issues (Estrella et al. 2000).

Figure 1. Sketch map of location of Yunnan and Guizhou in Southwest China (above) and project sites (below) (The boundaries and names shown on the maps in this publication do not imply official endorsement or acceptance by the International Development Research Centre.)

We hope that this book will fill a void by documenting the complete cycle of introduction, implementation, and assessment of a training approach in a real-life situation. It represents one of the first examples of this kind of effort in China, although the concept of PM&E is not new there (see Li Xiaoyun 2001: 115 – 128). This book, which is published in both English and Chinese, is aimed at a broad audience of practitioners and theoreticians interested in or involved with participatory research and development work, in China or elsewhere.

Opening a new window on research practice

More than anything, this book illustrates how PM&E has opened a new window on our research practice. Its integration into the project cycle has strengthened the learning, accountability, and effectiveness of the research efforts of the two teams, in particular through the realization that what matters is not only *what* is assessed, but *who* does the measuring and assessing. In addition, the experience gained during the PM&E activity has contributed to a better understanding of *how* different concerns and interests are represented and negotiated in a research process. The PM&E training and fieldwork contributed greatly to a better understanding by researchers and local government officials of the interests and needs of both women and men farmers. It also strengthened farmers' participation in the research process in Yunnan and Guizhou and catalyzed the introduction of a self-monitoring mechanism among farmers in Guizhou for the management of their local water system, thus enhancing local governance.

In the remainder of this chapter we describe how the PM&E experience was born and explain the capacity-building approach and process. This is followed by an introduction of the two projects, the organizations to which they belong, and a short description of the emergence and evolution of participatory research and development approaches in the southwest of China.

The interest in a PM&E process

The initiative to undertake a PM&E activity in China was born at the crossroads of two forces. On one track, the International Development Research Centre's (IDRC's) Community-Based Natural Resource Management (CBNRM) program promotes an interdisciplinary and participatory approach to solving problems related to natural resource management at the local level (see box). Building the research capacity necessary to apply this approach is an important goal of the program, and one component of this capacity – building concerns the monitoring and evaluation of research projects.

Community-Based Natural Resource Management in Asia

The Community-Based Natural Resource Management (CBNRM) program in Asia started in 1997 and builds on previous research supported by IDRC in the fields of agriculture, forestry, fisheries, and nutrition. The CBNRM program addresses the following issues.

Despite rapid industrialization and a well-established historical network of large cities, most people in Asia remain directly dependent on a productive natural resource base for their livelihoods. Unfortunately, pressures on this resource base are increasing (Rigg 1997). Urban-biased industrial development and non-locally managed international investments in export-oriented resource development are leading to resource degradation. Resettlement due to displacement, voluntary migration, and historical conflicts exacerbate these resource pressures. Rural populations have increased rapidly with the improvement of basic health and living conditions. This leads to an expansion of cultivated land, even into areas that are ecologically fragile or inappropriate for permanent cultivation. Within communities, power and gender relations often marginalize some social groups. Systems of resource tenure and access are complex, with traditional, culturally specific systems modified by colonial and state regulations that may be changing rapidly with national economic policy reforms.

Problems related to the sustainable management of natural resources are most critical in the uplands and coastal areas, where natural resource degradation can lead to irreversible loss of food productivity and the breakdown of ecosystems with loss of habitat. A widespread process in Asia is the privatization of natural resources such as forests and coastal areas that were previously collectively managed. Privatization may lead to productivity increases in the short term, but frequently it also increases poverty because poor people who previously had access to these resources are now excluded.

Although circumstances differ in different countries, there is a striking convergence of interest in questions of local resource management. Structural adjustment in some countries is leading to reductions in the technical and enforcement capability of the state. In others, major policy transitions are affecting all aspects of government interventions in the economy (Kristof and WuDunn 2000). External pressures due to expanding trade and investment and large-scale development projects in parts of the region previously isolated from international markets are also having a dramaticeffect on local resources. Local governments and grassroots organizations are, at the same time, becoming more assertive and articulate in their identification of resource questions — including the expression of their views and interests.

"Traditional" policies and research have often discounted the role of local people in the design and implementation of measures, projects, and programs. Proposing an alternative approach, the CBNRM program works with the local men and women most directly involved with natural resource management. Often they are the poorest of the rural poor or belong to ethnic minorities that are politically and economically isolated. The CBNRM program recognizes that these men and women may have intimate knowledge of the local resource base, may have (countervailing) views on resource use and management, and may be motivated to improve productivity if they can be assured of reaping the benefits (CBNRM 2000, http://www.idrc.ca/cbnrm).

On the other track, several of the research teams working with the CBNRM program identified PM&E as an important component of their research efforts, but lacked the necessary skills to integrate it into their projects (Vernooy 2001). In response to this interest, in early 1999 the CBNRM program team designed and funded a special project that aimed at addressing the need for improved research skills in PM&E. Ronnie Vernooy, a CBNRM team member and program officer based in Ottawa (and a rural development sociologist by training), collected and designed training materials and methods and facilitated the training process. The core elements of these are described below.

The approach and process

Training for PM&E is based on learning-by-doing and interaction, and consisted of a series of three workshops combined with fieldwork to strengthen conceptual and methodological skills (see Appendix 1 for an outline of the workshops).

The activity described here can best be viewed as a "pilot project" involving only two teams working with the CBNRM program: the Kunming Institute of Botany (KIB) /Chinese Academy of Sciences-PARDYP team in Kunming ("People and Resource Dynamics in Mountainous Watersheds" project); and the Guizhou Academy of Agricultural Sciences (GAAS) team in Guiyang ("CBNRM in the Mountainous Areas of Guizhou" project).

The objective was to design and implement a PM&E component that would complement ongoing research in both projects. The workshop format allowed participants not only to acquire conceptual and methodological insights into PM&E, but also to put them into practice immediately. Exchanging experiences between the teams allowed for critical reflection and revision of the PM&E component as required.

Workshop 1, Guiyang, Guizhou province, 20 – 23 July 1999

The first workshop introduced the key concepts, approach, and basic questions related to PM&E. The focus was very much on working toward a shared understanding of the meaning of participation, monitoring, and evaluation. The meeting brought the two teams together for the first time and allowed them to start exchanging ideas, experiences, and interests. The workshop also generated a draft PM&E plan for each team, focusing on a specific project component: water resource management in the case of the Guizhou team; and technology development with a focus on community management of tree nurseries in the case of the Kunming team. The key element in the elaboration of these draft plans was not so much the content (and topic chosen), but the process used to design them.

Workshop 2, Kunming, Yunnan province, 6 – 8 April 2000

The second workshop focused on the PM&E fieldwork carried out so far within the context of the projects at large. Both teams presented their research and PM&E work, highlighting what they had learned so far. They also provided feedback to each other through a "market" exercise: what would they "buy" (i.e., adopt) from each other, and what would they do differently. This proved to be very valuable. It was followed by exercises identifying and discussing research gaps linked to the six key PM&E questions: why? for whom? what? who? when? how? (more about these in chapter 2). Here the focus was on achieving a better sociological understanding of participation as a process. In small groups, the most important of the identified gaps were debated and suggestions were made for additional research work. The workshop was very intense and involved good exchange dynamics-an excellent example of CBNRM networking in practice.

Workshop 3, Baoshan, Yunnan province, 31 May to 2 June 2001

Additional and updated results of the fieldwork were presented and discussed at the third workshop, and a critical assessment of the overall experience was made through identification of the value added by the PM&E work, challenges and constraints, and possible next steps at both the project and organizational levels. The two teams also assessed the training method and made suggestions for improvement. In chapters 3 to 5, we present the results of the implementation of the training approach in the form of two case studies. In chapter 6, we reflect on achievements and shortcomings.

Key elements in capacity-building for PM&E

Two elements are central to PM&E capacity-building: access or the opportunity to take part in the process, and ability or the knowledge and skill to do something (Johnson 2000: 217 – 228). To ensure both access and ability in the capacity – building process, we designed the following chain of events (sometimes called theory of action, adapted from Patton 1997: 215 – 238).

1. Resources are devoted to monitoring and evaluation, including stakeholder time and financial inputs.
2. Working with intended users, important monitoring and evaluation issues and questions are defined, and, based on these, the design is prepared and data are collected.

3. Key stakeholders and primary users are involved throughout the process.
4. Intended users react to their involvement.
5. The monitoring and evaluation process and findings provide (new) knowledge and understanding.
6. Intended users interpret results, generate and adopt recommendations, and use the monitoring and evaluation results.
7. The project improves and (new) decisions are made.

The work described in this book involves two regional, well-established research organizations, both active in the area of natural-resource management and both supported by IDRC's CBNRM program (both organizations also receive funds from other donors, such as the Ford Foundation). In both cases, the PM&E component was added to ongoing research efforts. In both provinces, the whole project research team took part in the PM&E capacity-building process (although over time, some staff changes took place, notably in the GAAS team when several members went abroad to study) as well as a number of selected local people (farmers, technical staff, and government employees). Both teams also had strong organizational support when they undertook the PM&E process.

The idea of bringing the two teams together — from different organizations, with a different composition (age, men to women ratio, disciplinary background, experience), operating in different local contexts although with certain similarities in terms of natural resource management issues, but with a similar research focus and methodological approach — arose from the assumption that *two know more than one*. Learning from each other could increase effectiveness (as we would be able to learn about two cases simultaneously by comparing experiences), relevance (it would allow to see our own research in a broader context), and possibly efficiency (increased speed of learning).

As much as possible, we built on existing skills and relied on participants' contributions in a learning-by-doing, semi-structured process (rather than a blueprint training model) and a longer-term commitment based on the belief that a one-off event does not work in participatory research. For maximum utility, the workshops were conducted mainly in Chinese, with translation back and forth to English when necessary (during the first workshop by a Canadian-Chinese cofacilitator, during the second and third workshops by team members).

Resources used in the process included a binder of selected, background reading materials (compiled by Ronnie Vernooy) although no lectures about these materials were prepared; funds from IDRC for the organization of the three workshops; ongoing field research operations (PM&E fieldwork expenses were covered by project funds); and facilitation by Ms. Fong Ku (at the first workshop) and Ronnie Vernooy (at all three workshops). For workshops 1 and 2, the facilitator(s) prepared a number of hands-on exercises that occupied most of the time. In addition, several "ice-breaker" and energizing exercises were conducted to allow participants to look at PM&E from a different angle!

Overall, we aimed at an approach that Robert Chambers (1997: 214) has described as "inventive through interaction, practical in application, rigorous through self-criticism, and empowering through process." In the final chapter, we reflect on how well we did in putting this approach into practice and following the envisioned chain of events.

The project teams

Kunming Institute of Botany and the PARDYP team, Yunnan

The introduction of participatory methods in Yunnan: Before 1990, efforts to alleviate poverty and develop rural areas of China consisted largely of research projects and studies that had a limited policy orientation. Researchers collected data from (at best) lower levels of government and, rarely, carried out surveys or used other techniques at the community level. Findings were transmitted to policymakers, accompanied by comments and suggestions. Important decisions would be made, although not necessarily in compliance with study findings and recommendations. In the late 1980s and early 1990s, several factors contributed to a questioning of this modus operandi. New approaches began to surface. New centres and organizations emphasized the need to work toward "sustainable development" and highlighted the importance of involving people and communities in the development process. Yunnan province has been at the forefront of these changes.

Yunnan attracted the attention of international and nongovernmental organizations (NGOs), not only because it is one of the undeveloped provinces in China, but also because of the relatively open attitude of government officials toward innovative approaches (including those initiated by NGOs) and new sources of funding. A number of events set the wheels turning. The most significant was the development and approval of the Yunnan Upland Management Project, the first interdisciplinary, intersectoral collaborative project for integrated upland development. The project, which started in 1990 with funding and support from the Ford Foundation, was aimed at achieving sustainable development in the region. Project objectives included strengthening the capacity for interdisciplinary research and establishing a participatory approach to assessment, planning, and implementation. The capacity-building process began with a month-long social science training workshop on rural surveys, conducted by Nancy Peluso early in 1990. This was followed by training in rapid rural appraisal (RRA) by the Southeast Asian Universities Agroecosystem Research Network led by Dr. Percy Sajise. In 1993, additional training in participatory rural appraisal (PRA) was provided by Robert Chambers. After the PRA workshop, a number of practitioners and researchers decided to establish the Yunnan PRA Network based at the Rural Development Research Centre to look at ways to apply these methods in the Chinese context.

The Yunnan Upland Management Project: In 1987, the Yunnan Poverty Alleviation Office (YPAO) asked the Yunnan Academy of Social Sciences (YASS) to carry out a study called "Strategy for Poverty Alleviation and Economic Development of 41 Poor Counties in Yunnan." At about the same time, representatives of the Ford Foundation China and Winrock International Asian Regional Office conducted a study tour in Yunnan. Two major causes of poverty identified in an earlier study were lack of information and lack of qualified staff owing to the remoteness of Yunnan. Following discussions with the head of the YPAO and the director of the Institute of Rural Economy (at YASS), the two donors agreed to cooperate with the provincial government on the Yunnan Upland Management Demonstration Project.

This project focused on four counties, each representing a poverty classification type. In each county, one village was selected as a project demonstration site. Project participants — including researchers and teachers from both the natural and social sciences, as well as government officials — from 13 organizations had the opportunity to spend long periods of time working with the villagers at the grassroots level. Their experience made them realize the importance of farmers' participation in decision-making (Assessment Working Group 1998).

Between 1991 and 1994, 30 people from the various participating units were sent to selected universities in Thailand and the Philippines for training in environmental sciences, natural resource management, social forestry, agricultural systems, social and development studies, and other related areas. In 1995, 13 more people were chosen and, since then, Winrock International has sponsored new participants each year. In Kunming, training was provided in English, RRA, PRA, interviewing skills, and monitoring and evaluation; these skills were then put into practice at the demonstration sites.

This program has created a group of high-quality trainees, many of whom have established their own NGOs or participated in international projects in Yunnan province by providing feasibility reports and consultancy services.

The Yunnan PRA Network: In 1993, the Yunnan Institute of Geography invited Robert Chambers to provide training in PRA. The result was the establishment of the Yunnan PRA Network in 1994 (mainly funded by the Ford Foundation, with a small initial grant from the Institute of Development Studies, University of Sussex). Since then, participatory approaches in Yunnan have largely been promoted and applied by members of that network, through their own research and action projects, through their participation in government projects, or through consultancy services they have provided to international agencies.

The network has provided many training experiences to its 52 members, as well as opportunities to practice their new skills through the allocation of small grants. Most of its members see the network as a forum of people with a common interest and value its relaxed atmosphere in which information is exchanged and interdisciplinary sharing stimulated.

After several years of learning by doing and sharing, most network members praise the benefits of participatory methods and have tried to adopt them in their daily work. They believe that cooperation among equals and mutual understanding and trust should be important components of any development initiative, as they are necessary to build harmonious and productive working relations between villagers and outsiders. Experimenting with participatory methods has changed the attitudes of project staff and local officials toward farmers and made them realize the capabilities of the latter. Villagers, on the other hand, have gained confidence and awareness of their role in self-development, which, in turn, has increased their interest and enthusiasm.

The participatory process has often been accompanied by a change of roles. Farmers take on more responsibility as they actively participate in decisions regarding projects that will affect their lives. Meanwhile, government agencies can focus more on providing services and training, ensuring organizational structure, assisting farmers, and providing information. In research projects, respect and transparent working procedures have also significantly contributed to the generation and sharing of information.

One issue that has been stressed by members of the PRA Network and thoroughly discussed during meetings is the importance of institutional structures and supporting project management mechanisms that enable and support participation. Many innovations in that direction have been implemented, as "the establishment of community organizational institutions and structures are an important basis of sustainable community production, livelihoods and development management ···, Community organizational management and coordination capacities are often ignored in the provision of external support. Thus, in some projects after the project ends, all the achievements and progress cannot be sustained" (Xue Jinling, quoted in Wilkes 2000). For example, one project developed a system to monitor the use of participatory methods in its design process. In another case, technicians had to report to villagers and seek their approval for any changes in technical designs. There are many other experiments of this kind.

However, in many instances, the lack of such supporting mechanisms has presented an important obstacle to the implementation of participatory methods. Many PRA practitioners in Yunnan come from research institutes whose mandate is mainly to provide consulting services and training, but not to implement projects. Thus, even if they use participatory tools in the design of projects and activities, top-down implementation and management styles prevent the continuation of the participation. Moreover, the leaders of many institutes do not recognize PRA as a valid research method, let alone its promotion as a mission. This situation creates a conflict for practitioners whose work units relate promotion and salary bonuses to the number of "valid" research reports published. There is thus a real need to train project implementers and field staff in participatory project management to reconcile participatory project tools and approaches with appropriate management structures.

Participatory approaches also require a gradual learning process on the part of villagers, local staff, and government officials. This is especially true in China, where farmers are used to being told what to do by government officials and, thus, need time to begin trusting outsiders who are questioning the status quo. If insufficient time and consideration are given to gradual learning, passive participation may result despite the adoption of participatory approaches. On the other hand, where gradual learning is allowed, participatory approaches prove to be better adapted to local conditions and the uncritical use of methods can be avoided. The cost of this approach, especially in terms of manpower, presents a significant limitation (Lu Xing 2000; Wilkes 2000).

The Kunming Institute of Botany: In 1987, the KIB established a Department of Ethnobotany to promote the investigation, documentation, and evaluation of indigenous knowledge systems related to useful plants and herbal medicines; to conserve the great wealth of biological and cultural diversity of southwest China; and to promote socially equitable and environmentally sound development in the mountainous ethnic minority areas of that region.

It is the first department of a research institute in Yunnan to carry out fieldwork and interdisciplinary research. Participatory methods were initially introduced through projects — the first instance was in the early 1990s during the implementation of the "Rehabilitation of Degraded Lands of Mountainous Ecosystems in the Hindu-Kush Himalayas" project, funded by IDRC. Later, in 1993, after four members of the department attended the already mentioned PRA training course facilitated by Robert Chambers, they applied PRA to their community-based biodiversity conservation and community development projects. Other staff members were exposed to participatory methods through joint fieldwork and training opportunities offered by the newly created Yunnan PRA Network. Most of the department's staff joined the network's forestry group, which was headed by Xu Jianchu, the deputy head of the department and the PARDYP country coordinator.

Through the implementation of participatory methods, the work of the Department of Ethnobotany progressively shifted from quantitative research focusing on data collection to applied ethnobotany for community development. Eventually, the department adopted the framework of participatory technology development (PTD) to direct most of its work in the field.

PTD requires long-term interaction between outsiders and local people; its aim is to develop sustainable systems of livelihood based on indigenous/local knowledge and cultures. It links the power and capacity of agricultural research with the interests and the knowledge of local communities. In a broader sense, PTD deals with natural resources management by strengthening the local, indigenous specialists and their communities and enabling them to carry out experiments to become more sustainable and self-reliant using their local resources. Development practitioners recognize themselves as "outsiders" in the rural environment and should, therefore,

- focus on creative interactions within rural communities so that indigenous knowledge and local experiences become the driving force of development;

- be aware that their own knowledge is the product of learning at research centres, universities and development agencies and is technical/scientific/modern knowledge;
- promote dialogue between the two knowledge systems to find joint solutions to rural problems, taking full advantage of local resources (natural, social, and cultural).

The role of outsiders, thus, consists of facilitating the intercultural process of learning and sharing between the "technicians" from development institutions and local people, as well as facilitating the organization of a network of village specialists that will increase communication about local innovations and encourage local people to continue experimenting with new forms of self-sustaining agriculture and resource management (more about the PTD process in chapter 3).

Although independent in many ways, as part of a formal research institute, the Department of Ethnobotany has also recognized the shortcomings of some aspects of its managerial structure and has recently taken steps to overcome them. In particular, the "People and Resource Dynamics in Mountainous Watersheds" project (PARDYP) has provided an opportunity for learning and experimenting with PM&E.

The "People and Resource Dynamics in Mountainous Watersheds" project: PARDYP is a research-for-development project, initiated in October 1996 with funds from the Swiss Agency for Development and Cooperation (SDC), IDRC, and the International Center for Integrated Mountain Development (ICIMOD), with the aim to contribute to a balanced, sustainable and equitable development of mountain communities and families in the Hindu-Kush Himalayas (HKH). Five watersheds with different characteristics were selected in Nepal (two watersheds), China, India, and Pakistan to learn some of the issues involved in managing their resources and, with the participation of local people, develop means of improving this management. In China, KIB coordinates research in the Xizhuang watershed (Baoshan city) in close collaboration with a number of government departments.

The objectives of phase I of the project, which was completed at the end of 1999, were:

- to generate relevant and representative information about , and technologies for, measuring water balance and sediment transport related to degradation in a watershed;
- to identify technologies and strategies to improve soil fertility and control erosion and degradation using a farming system approach;
- to generate socioeconomic information on resource management and degradation;
- to apply community-based participatory principles in the generation, testing, and evaluation of natural resource management strategies and technology;
- to strengthen participation of project partners;
- to make relevant information on project outputs accessible to stakeholders;
- to manage the project, effectively and efficiently, as a regional collaborative research and development project.

During phase I, participants made a start at understanding many of the issues involved in the management (and degradation) of resources by communities and, with the help of local people, began introducing means of improving natural resource management (Allen et al. 2000). However, the emphasis during the first 3 years was on biophysical research. Although a wealth of technical data were collected, more effort is needed to move from research to development, and to turn the technical and social understanding of physical resource dynamics into appropriate natural resources management strategies that contribute to the improvement of local people's livelihoods.

Thus, the objectives of phase II initiated in 2000, are:

- to build on and generate knowledge and facilitate the exchange and dissemination of information and skills in the middle mountains of the Hindu-Kush Himalayas;
- to enhance the capacities and options of families and communities,

especially those who are marginalized, in the use and management of natural resources in mountain watersheds, thereby increasing household and community benefits;

● to stimulate and engage in wide-ranging policy dialogues through the involvement of policymakers at local and higher levels in the research activities and in the development needs of people in the four project countries.

The project cycle now includes cycles of participatory planning and implementation, accompanied by rounds of PM&E (Fig. 2). Throughout the whole process, the responsibilities of the PARDYP team should diminish from their initial leading role to an accompaniment function, and finally retreat. Steps

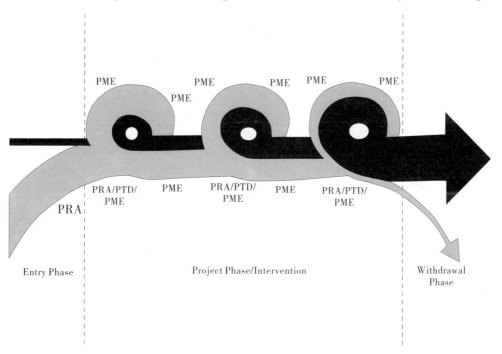

Figure 2. The PARDYP project cycle. The *light* indicates the PARDYP team; *the black*, the local people; the thickness of these lines reflects the relative responsibility of these two groups during the various phases. PME = participatory monitoring and evaluation; PRA = participatory rural appraisal; PTD = participatory technology development.

will be taken to turn over responsibilities to local people and empower and motivate them to initiate their own activities.

For this reason, the entry and withdrawal phases are extremely important. During the entry phase, identifying and building good relations with local partners is key, and this requires making the project mission and methods clear to all the various stakeholders. At that point, the specific goals of the project will be developed together with the local communities, who should be in agreement about the work. The withdrawal phase includes building the capacity of local organizations or institutions to continue supporting the initiatives developed by local people. This is necessary for the sustainability of project interventions.

The Guizhou Academy of Agricultural Sciences and Community-based Natural Resources Management project team, Guizhou

The Guizhou Academy of Agricultural Sciences: The GAAS is the provincial governmental body of the Chinese Academy of Agricultural Sciences. It carries out research in agriculture, horticulture, soils and water management, conservation, and, since the beginning of the 1990s, community-based natural resource management. Funding for research comes from the Chinese government and through a number of donor-funded projects, such as IDRC's CBNRM project. Other donors include the Canadian International Development Agency (CIDA), the Ford Foundation, and the Asian Development Bank. In 2000, the team that carried out the IDRC-funded project created a new unit at the GAAS, named the Integrated Rural Development Centre (IRDC; not to confuse with IDRC).

The IRDC is committed to the sustainable development of rural Guizhou through the effective, efficient, and equitable use of limited natural resources. It advocates a participatory approach to policy changes, provides training and extension for local capacity-building, and raises research and development funds for the adaptation of methods and technologies that contribute to sustainable community development and poverty alleviation. The first director of the new centre is Ms. Sun Qiu.

Following the example of Yunnan, a number of researchers from GAAS and other organizations in Guizhou province established the Guizhou Participatory Rural Appraisal Network. Currently, the network has over 30 members with backgrounds in agriculture, ecology, forestry, sociology, anthropology, and management. The Ford Foundation and the CIDA's Canada Fund provide financial support. The network and its members are involved in internal capacity-building, training, consultancies, and project implementation, monitoring, and evaluation. Four theme groups make up the network: conservation and community development, social forestry, natural resource management, and ethnicity, gender and development.

The CBNRM project: Guizhou, located in the southwest, is also one of the undeveloped provinces in China and about half its population belongs to ethnic minority groups. These groups mainly inhabit the mountainous rural areas where they manage complex production systems consisting of irrigated and rainfed rice fields, less-productive uplands and grasslands, forested areas and so-called "wastelands." Problems that people face include low yields, little crop diversification, forests that in general are not in good health, and overgrazed common grasslands.

In 1995, a multidisciplinary research team at the GAAS initiated research in two villages, Dabuyang and Xiaozhai in Changsuan county, to address natural resource management issues at the local level. Using participatory appraisal tools, the team described and analyzed current household and community-based management practices, evaluated the impact of economic, sociocultural and agro-ecological factors on the natural resource base in the villages, and identified constraints and opportunities for technical and policy interventions aimed at improving livelihoods and the sustainable management of land, water and trees (Chen Deshou et al. 2000).

With input from and the participation of villagers, the team facilitated the implementation of the following interventions and monitored and evaluated their impact.

- Management groups and rules and regulations for resource use and management were established. The rules and regulations were based on the customary laws of the local communities, and the members of the management groups were selected by village assemblies. To date, the resource management organizations at the community level have been effective, because they are relevant to real situations and are operated by the local farmers. They complement the state laws.
- Participation of the local farmers in resource management was enhanced through participatory planning and implementation of the project, and PM&E activities.
- Capacities of local communities were increased through various training activities, cross-farm visits, and fieldwork.
- PTD was practiced; farming technology options were provided and tested in farmers' fields by farmers and researchers.
- A participatory model of infrastructure-building at the community level was designed focusing on integrating livelihood improvements and innovative management processes. Women and men farmers were involved in the design, mobilization of resources (labour, materials, and funds), construction, operations, and maintenance. The meaningful involvement of the local farmers in the whole process has been the key incentive for building high-quality facilities and managing them well (with an eye for efficiency, equity, and sustainability).

In one village, a 200-year-old problem was solved by the construction of a village-managed drinking water system, which is regulated under a set of standards and rules that define the rights and obligations of all users (more about water management in chapter 4). New regulations for the management of the remaining, collectively owned forest lands were formulated in both villages and include an obligation to practice afforestation and reforestation. Orchards were established on some of the wastelands. Physicians and health care workers from GAAS also spent time in the two villages; their support was of particular benefit to women and children.

Following a very positive external evaluation of the project in 1998, a proposal for a second phase was developed and approved by IDRC. The principal aim of the second phase was to investigate opportunities for the transfer of the approach and its results to four new villages and, eventually, to the whole province. At the same time, the team continued to monitor health, nutrition, and environmental conditions in Dabuyang and Xiaozhia villages. In the four new villages, participatory analyses of resource management systems, including the study of gender roles, were carried out and constraints and opportunities for interventions were identified. The research team also broadened the involvement of key stakeholders, actively including local and provincial-level administrators and policymakers. In addition, the team integrated PM&E concepts and tools into the research cycle to reflect critically on the research process and the meaning of participation. This further strengthened learning and increased accountability and effectiveness because PM&E emphasizes not only *what* is being monitored and evaluated, but also *who* is measuring and *how* various concerns and interests are negotiated and represented (Sun Qiu et al. 2000).

The KIB-PARDYP and GAAS-CBNRM projects are good example of learning-by-doing; team members were trained to use a set of new tools, then went on to develop and adapt a participatory, integrated natural and social science approach to address community-based institutional and management issues together with farmers. "Working for our own dreams," is how the farmers describe this process. In the following chapters we document in more detail how these capacity building and research efforts are contributing to the realization of their dreams.

2. Building a common understanding: core concepts and methods

Utilization-focused questions are of direct personal interest to identified and organized decision-makers and information users. They want to answer the question for themselves, not for someone else: they personally care about the answer to the question. The reason for identifying and organizing relevant decision-makers and information users is to be sure that the people who are going to be the primary users of the evaluation findings are the same people who decide what the focus of the evaluation will be. This means that the evaluation should focus on their information needs-not on their speculations about what someone else wants to know. (Patton 1978:87)

In this chapter, we build on the concepts, ideas, and tools described in two documents produced by IDRC's Community-Based Natural Resource Management program: Understanding participation: monitoring and evaluating process, outputs and outcomes, by Karen McAllister (1999) and Action and reflection: a guide for monitoring and evaluating participatory research, by Karen McAllister and Ronnie Vernooy (1999). Throughout this chapter, we include examples of the exercises used at the three training workshops to illustrate how both project teams implemented and reflected on the central concepts, questions and methods based on their ongoing fieldwork in Yunnan and Guizhou and based on previous research and training experiences. (Note: an introduction and descriptions of all the exercises can be found in Appendix 2.) We stress the importance of building, through the iterative process of training workshops and fieldwork, a common understanding of what PM&E is all about among team members and others involved in the research process. Our experience shows that a joint team approach to learning, combined with an ongoing process that includes concrete training exercises and fieldexperience, can be instrumental in achieving this.

Defining participatory, monitoring, and evaluation

Participatory (i.e., participation or taking part in) means various types and degrees of involvement, control over and decision-making in an activity (or a research process). It can encompass a wide range of approaches, methods, and tools, and debates abound in the literature. The rationale for using a participatory process may be functional: to encourage participation to increase the usefulness (i.e., relevance and effectiveness) of the research to stakeholders or users or to increase the efficiency of the process, or both. Another reason may be empowerment or social transformation: participation as both a means and an end to strengthen local people's capacity to make decisions and their ability to create an environment for change. Often, participation has both functional and empowering aspects, and the types and degrees of participation change during the project cycle or research process. Thus, it is crucial to ask the questions: *whose* participation? and participation in *what*?

Monitoring is the systematic, regular collection and occasional analysis of information to identify and possibly measure changes over a period of time. *Evaluation* is the analysis of the effectiveness and direction of an activity or research project and involves making a judgement about progress and impact. The main differences between monitoring and evaluation are the timing and frequency of observations and the types of questions asked. However, when monitoring and evaluation are integrated into a research strategy as a project management tool, the line between the two becomes rather blurred. PM&E is the *joint effort or partnership* of two or more stakeholders (such as researchers, farmers, government officials, extension workers) to monitor and evaluate, systematically, one or more research or development activities.

PM&E has emerged because of recognition of the limitations of conventional monitoring and evaluation (Table 1). Conventional monitoring and evaluation mainly serve the needs of project implementers and donors and ignore the interests of other groups involved in research and development efforts, especially local people. These activities are normally carried out by outside "experts," with the result that a gap exists between the experts' perception of the project and its results and that of the people who are directly involved. In addition, monitoring and evaluation are usually done toward the end of a program or project, allowing little opportunity for improvement during early and mid-term implementation.

In contrast, PM&E emphasizes participation of the stakeholders in deciding how project progress should be measured and results acted on. Broadening the involvement of the various stakeholders in identifying and analyzing change can create a clearer picture of what is really happening on the ground and can include the perspectives of women, men, and various age, class, and ethnic groups. It allows people to share successes and learn from each other. At the same time, PM&E is potentially very empowering, as it puts local people in charge, helps develop their skills, shows that their views count, and provides an opportunity for joint learning.

Table 1. Comparison of conventional monitoring and evaluation and PM&E

Key questions	Conventional	Participatory
Why?	Accountability	Adjustment in process Empowerment
What?	Predetermined indicators	Local indicators
Who?	External evaluators	Stakeholders Community members
For whom?	Donors, researchers	Stakeholders
When?	On completion	Frequent Regular
How?	External review Distanced approach Delayed, long report	Self-evaluation Simple tools Direct results

PM&E is not only a monitoring and evaluation exercise, but also, more important, it increases the accountability of all the people involved and allows for capacity-building and empowerment of the local communities. This, in turn, can lead to more promising or successful projects and programs. PM&E is an integral component of a project and is closely woven into the whole project cycle (although not necessarily used in all project components or activities). It provides information that can be fed back into the project immediately to improve subsequent performance.

It is important to be aware that the results generated by participatory research, and thus by PM&E, depend on the context in which the research takes place: socioeconomic and political situation; local culture; resource access and rights; social identities and relationships along lines of gender, class, kinship, ethnicity, and age; and attitudes, interests, and abilities of the various stakeholders including the researchers (e.g., their understanding of community dynamics, gender and social relations). In other words, as with all science, we need to be aware that knowledge is socially structured and that this implies a process of representation, discussion, and potential conflict and negotiation (Long and Long 1992).

Exercise (from the first workshop)
Defining the core concepts participatory, monitoring, and evaluation

Plenary session: Please describe what the core concepts of participatory (participation), monitoring and evaluation mean to you. Use short descriptions or key words.

Results
Participatory or participation means

- The sharing of experiences and lessons with others; recognizing that all stakeholders have responsibilities, obligations, and accountabilities and can benefit from the activities.
- Democracy; researcher-farmer-technician-government staff involvement (multirole participation); beneficiary-centred, all the stakeholders are carrying out the project; everybody cares about the project; all the

stakeholders take part in the activities; joint participation.

Monitoring means

- Identifying problems, proposing adjustments and improvements of the project; rviewing the past, present, and future; measuring project implementation in terms of quality and quantity; adjusting project activities, expected results, and objectives continuously.
- Supervising; using indicators to assess the project from an outsider's view.
- All project members understand the whole process gradually; recording and assessing the whole implementation process; tracking and measuring progress.
- Examining whether predetermined objectives are achieved; examining project execution; measuring the gap between activities and objectives; examining and reviewing periodically.

Evaluation means

- Identifying the extent of the completion of objectives; integrated assessment of results according to objectives; examining whether the objectives are achieved; evaluating the outputs and impact of the project.
- Judging and reviewing whether project is successful; commenting; reviewing, examining.

Reflection

This exercise proved useful as a first attempt to define broadly the key concepts. The various connotations of monitoring and evaluation emerged, and essential elements of participation were identified. Building on the exercise, it was not difficult to highlight the main differences between conventional and participatory monitoring and evaluation as summarized in Table 1.

Exercise (from the second workshop)
Factors shaping the process of PM&E implementation

To understand the process of implementing PM&E, we need to look at the context in which we as researchers work. Please consider the following factors that shape the process and, based on your own field experience, review them by filling in the table presented below.

Results

Factor	Relevance	Enabling	Constraining	How to deal with factors?
Social aspects of natural resource management, such as values, norms, difference between men and women, occurrence of conflicts	Very important	Local rules and regulations (GAAS): could serve as a base for changes and improvements.	Local rules and regulations (GAAS): those with more power sometimes oppose changes. Conflicts between officials and households about benefit sharing (KIB).	Research team needs to learn about local institutions. Democratically elected village leaders. Open up village accounting books. Establishment of autonomous farmer experimental groups.
Attitudes of the researchers and their understanding of the local context	Very important		Researchers are often facing time constraints and this affects the way they operate.	Team training and learning. More practice. Sharing among team; regular review of work. Exchanges between researchers and farmers.

Factor	Relevance	Enabling	Constraining	How to deal with factors?
Perceptions of the local people about the research process	Very important	When research addresses important livelihood issues, farmers are usually keen to participate.	Negative past experiences can hamper interest and participation of farmers. Over time, interest may fade or some community members may "drop out."	Research should address actual problems and try to solve them. Involve farmers in decision-making about research steps. Train farmers. The attitudes and work styles of outsiders need to change.
Skills of the researchers and of the local people	Very important	Ideally, over time, local capacities should increase and local people should take on a stronger role in the research process.	Researchers need to be flexible and adapt and learn how to give more space to local people.	Regular reviewing, and sharing of information. More practice.

Reflection

This exercise generated lively discussion among the members of the two teams. It allowed us to stand back and reflect critically on our practice, i.e., on how we actually do things/get things done. The observations as presented in the table stress the factor time and the dynamic nature of building relationships with people in the communities.

The magic wheel of PM&E

Bearing these definitions of the core concepts in mind, we embrace a method that is organized around six basic, interrelated questions that need to be answered if the PM&E is to be sound. These questions are represented around the "magic wheel of PM&E" in Figure 3: why do we monitor and evaluate? for whom? what? who? when? and how will we do it?

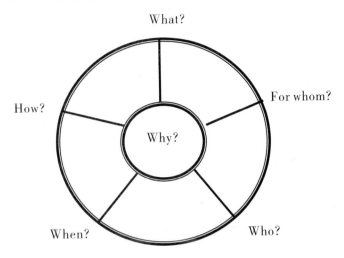

Figure 3. The magic wheel of PM&E

This method is **not** meant to be a blueprint, but, through specific issues related to each of the six questions, it makes an art of monitoring and evaluating participatory research. In our experience, the method captured by this seemingly simple wheel has proved useful throughout the whole process of integrating PM&E into the research process. We say seemingly simple, because the workshops and fieldwork activities served as a vivid reminder that wheels only turn well when spokes are solid and interconnected. Only then can we experience the "magic" of movement!

The interrelated answers to the six questions allow the development of a PM&E action plan and process, either at the project or the program (organizational) level. The stages in this process are captured in Figures 4 and 5. Both these figures resulted from a working group session on PM&E at the 2nd International Community-Based Natural Resource Management workshop, held in Guiyang, China, 12 – 16 October 2000, facilitated by Sun Qiu and Ronnie Vernooy (Vernooy 2001: 39). In the following section we discuss each of the six questions and related issues in more detail.

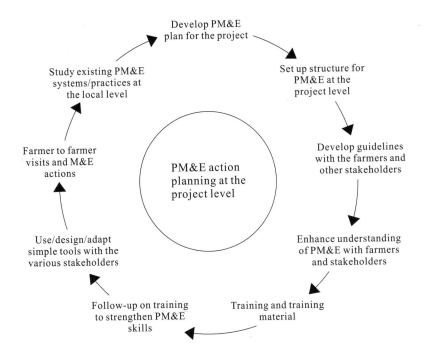

Figure 4. Stages in the PM&E action plan at the project level

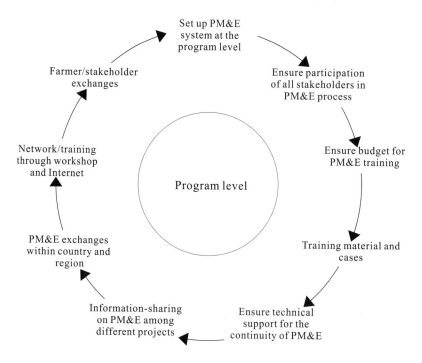

Figure 5. Stages in the PM&E action plan at the program level

Why? — defining the goals

In our judgment, the why question is central — thus, its position at the hub of the wheel. In general, according to Estrella and Gaventa (1998: 5), goals can be:

- To assess project results: to find out if objectives are being met and are resulting in desired changes.
- To improve project management and process planning: to better adapt to contextual and risk factors, such as social and power dynamics that affect the research process.
- To promote learning: to identify lessons of general applicability, to learn how different approaches to participation affect outcomes, impact, and reach, to learn what works and what doesn't, and to identify what contextual factors enable or constrain participatory research.
- To understand different stakeholders' perspectives: to allow, through direct participation in the monitoring and evaluation process, the various people involved in a research project to better understand each others views and values and to design ways to resolve competing or conflicting views and interests.
- To ensure accountability: to assess whether the project is effectively, appropriately, and efficiently executed to be accountable to they key agencies supporting the work (including, but not exclusively, the donors).

Usually, a monitoring and evaluation plan includes a combination of these goals, but it may be necessary to put more emphasis on one of them, depending on available resources, skills, and time and on the point in the project life-cycle during which the monitoring and evaluation will be done (see the section on when).

Exercise (from the first workshop)
Defining the goals of participatory monitoring and evaluation (why?)

Please list possible goals or aims of doing PM&E in a research project.

Results

	Why PM&E?
Objective	• To understand the execution and effects and be able to guarantee the project's success • To achieve better project results and impact • To improve project design • To achieve community benefits • To improve overall quality of the project and increasingly be able to conform to the people's wishes • To get feedback from local people about their views on the project's success (or failure)
Method	• The beneficiaries examine, adjust, and evaluate project process and results • To review, reflect on, and adjust activities • To understand the project process and existing problems, to be able to adjust research • To guarantee participation and equity in the project implementation process • To have local people participate in the whole project process
Other	• To formulate recommendations for future activities • To understand local natural resources and socioeconomic status

Reflection

The plenary brainstorming session produced this impressive list of goals, which the group divided into three types: related to project objectives; methods and participation (process); and "other." The two teams then turned to their own projects and listed the goal(s) in implementing PM&E and then went on to consider the other five questions (we have included the various related exercises in the following sections). Step by step, the teams designed a PM&E plan connecting each new step to the previous accomplished ones. The end results are captured in two project tables (Tables 2 and 3) that we include at the end of this chapter. In chapters 3, 4 and 5 we discuss how these plans were implemented in the field.

For whom? — identifying the users

As Patton so aptly stated, it is of little value to carry out a monitoring or evaluation process if no one is going to use the results, i.e., if no one cares. Therefore, identifying and involving or engaging users is a key step in the process. The main users of PM&E can include donor agencies, programs, researchers, research institutions, policymakers, government units, and communities (differentiated according to age, class, ethnicity etc.). A coherent definition of the users is important because different stakeholders often have different interests and, therefore, different information and evaluation requirements. For example, researchers may be interested in monitoring to influence decisions about research design, whereas donors may be more interested in accountability (did the project accomplish what it planned to and, if not, why not?). Villagers may have other interests altogether and among villagers there may be different interests and viewpoints as well.

Changes resulting from participatory research projects can be considered for various types of stakeholders who have been involved in and affected by the research process:

- *For researchers and research institutions*: Has their research capacity improved? *Whose* capacity? Do they have a better understanding of participatory processes? *Whose* understanding?
- *For community and groups within the community*: Are they using more equitable decision-making processes? Are their natural resource

management systems improved? Have their livelihoods improved? *Whose processes, systems, livelihoods?*

- **For policymakers**: Have their attitudes and behaviour toward local involvement in resource management changed? Are they more open to involving local people in decision-making? *Which* local people?

Therefore, we recommend identifying from the very beginning the main user(s) in terms of the PM&E rationale (why?) and what changes are important to measure for whom.

Exercise (from the first workshop)
Identifying the "beneficiaries" of PM&E (for whom?)

Please define clearly for whom you would do the PM&E. Be as specific as possible, for example, when answering "for the community," explain for whom in the community?

Results
See Tables 2 and 3 at the end of the chapter.

What? — defining the object

The choice of what to monitor and evaluate is closely linked to the question "for whom?" and ideally these should be defined together. When considering what to look at in an evaluation, it is useful to distinguish among the various kinds of results generated from the research — the outputs, processes, outcomes, and impacts — and to consider each. In the following paragraphs we briefly define these important concepts.

Outputs include the research activities themselves (the steps in the process) as well as the tangible products of the research. Outputs include information, such as a profile of a community, documentation of indigenous knowledge of plant species or local management practices, and so on organized in a report, for example. Outputs also include products, such as new techniques or technologies developed through farmer experimentation, new management regimes for common resources, new community institutions and organizations, or community development plans. Measures such as the number of people trained, the number of farmers involved in on-farm experiments, and the number of reports or publications of the research are also considered to be outputs. For evaluation purposes, it is important to move beyond assessing the mere production of outputs (whether activities occurred or certain products materialized) and to consider also the quality (what was the nature of the activities? were all those interested in the project able to participate? are the outputs useful? for whom? and so on).

Processes encompass the approach and methods used. PM&E can increase understanding of how these shape research results, including the more intangible outcomes, such as capacity-building and empowerment. Elements of processes include the critical analysis of the limitations and benefits of tools; awareness of the power and social relations that underlie participatory processes and influence whose perspectives are presented; and insights into how participatory methods and the context in which they are used influence resulting information and actions. Key participatory process issues that must be monitored and evaluated include:

- The *quality* of the information, participation, and representation, including the effectiveness of the methods and tools for enabling participation, representation, community capacity-building and ownership of the process, and for generating the desired research results. The representation and genuine participation of various stakeholders can be monitored and documented. Indicators of representation can include quantitative information such as how many people or who attended meetings. However, monitoring should also include such relevant qualitative information as who is vocal, a brief critical description of the social dynamics of the event (especially conflicts), and information about how decisions are made, how conflicts are managed, and whose interests are served through the research process.

- The *relevance* of the participatory approach to the goals of the research, including the type of participatory research and level of community control over the process and the ability of researchers to apply and adapt the methods to the local situation and needs. It also implies that the researchers make an effort to include the number and kinds of stakeholders necessary for the project to be effective (e.g., involving government officials if changing their policies is important for the research to have an influence).

- The *potential of the process to lead to reliable results*. Ways to verify this (Pretty 1995), include:
    - Prolonged or intensive contact between the researchers and local people to build trust and better understanding of the research context and local social dynamics and institutions.
    - Triangulation of process and results by using different methods or by having different researchers collect the same information.
    - Cross - checking the results of participatory research with local participants to ensure validity, and involvement of local people in the analysis of results to ensure that the views represented are really those of the local people.
    - Peer or external review of results and the research process.
    - Detailed documentation of the research process (e . g ., through diaries).
    - Reports that include contextual descriptions and quotations from local people to capture the complex social reality and include multiple local perspectives and experiences.

- *The potential of the participatory process to lead to local empowerment or social transformation*. Establishing the goal of social transformation implies that the central issue in participatory research is not the tools, but control over the process of knowledge generation and use. Researchers must consciously promote the gradual shift of control over the research process into the hands of the community. When considering the potential of the research in this direction, it is also important to consider representation to understand how the research has contributed to shifting power dynamics within the community. Empowerment can be measured by the degree to which local people or a specific group have:

- Improved capacity (knowledge, problem-solving skills, etc.) to deliberate about choices of action;
- Reports that include contextual descriptions and quotations from local people to capture the complex social reality and include multiple local perspectives and experiences;
- Broader options for concrete action; and
- Increased autonomy to carry out these options.

An important component of empowerment at the community level is strengthening social capital or the shared and built up knowledge (vision), skills, practices and institutions of local/indigenous people. This includes strengthening communications between people within the community as well as between community members and outside groups (such as the government, NGOs, other communities), and strengthening local organizations and institutions so that communities are better able to act collectively.

Participatory research methods can be monitored and evaluated based on their contribution to strengthening community capacity to establish how different participatory activities generate awareness, knowledge, attitudes, and skills; whether this learning is locally retained; the influence of the learning on those not directly involved in the activity; whether the learning changes local behaviour and norms in terms of how things are done; and the resilience of these behavioural transformations (Robinson et al. 1997:812).

Donor agencies are often interested in how the research process has affected researchers and research institutions, as well as local communities. At the researcher level, the transformative effects of participatory research can be considered with regard to whether researchers' capacity to work with communities has increased, whether their attitudes toward local knowledge have changed, and whether they are integrating participatory approaches into other research activities.

Outcomes are the changes — within the community or among the researchers — that can be attributed, at least in part, to the research process. Outcomes result both from meeting research objectives (outputs) and from the participatory research process itself. They can be negative or positive, expected or unexpected, and encompass both the functional effects of participatory research (e.g., greater adoption and diffusion of new technologies, changed farming practices, changes in institutions or management regimes) and the empowering effects (e.g., increased community capacity, improved confidence or self-esteem, and improved ability to resolve conflict or solve problems). The desired outcomes of participatory research in natural resource management projects generally involve social transformation; many are diffuse, long term, and notoriously difficult to measure or to attribute to a particular research project or activity.

Impact concerns the changes that occur in the community, where the research project is one of many contributing factors. Suffice it to say that it is usually difficult to clearly attribute the impact of a participatory research project. Desired impacts can be sustainability of livelihoods and natural resources, empowerment of communities, decreased poverty, and improved equity. Because overall development impacts are often observable only in the long term and are influenced by many factors external to the project, it is more realistic for evaluation purposes to consider outcomes as intermediate signs of impact.

Reach refers to who is influenced (by the research) and who acts because of this influence. Reach is closely related to the concept of equity. Participatory research is assumed to improve reach to disadvantaged groups and communities by including them in defining research priorities and capacity-building activities, and by mobilizing them to act in their own interests, rather than treating them as passive objects intended to benefit from the research results.

In practice, differentiating between process, output, outcomes, and reach can be difficult. For example, an output such as a community plan can become an input to the establishment of a community organization, which can be considered either as an output of the research or an outcome of the plan. Therefore, it is important to consider the appropriate time-line when looking at what to monitor and evaluate. This points to the importance of understanding the situation (e.g., a community differentiated by social factors) before the project is initiated. A clear view of the current state will provide a point of comparison when monitoring and evaluating changes that occur during the project. Participatory baseline analysis, conducted at the beginning of the project, can provide such a point of reference.

Exercise (from the first workshop)
Defining the objectives of PM&E (what?)

Please define the possible objective(s) of PM&E in your project. If you list more than one objective, please try to rank them in order of importance. Explain the reason(s) for your selection.

Results
See Tables 2 and 3 at the end of the chapter.

Indicators are easily measurable or observable criteria that provide information about changes in specific conditions that cannot be easily measured or observed. Proxy indicators substitute for indicators that cannot be assessed directly (for example, when it is difficult to obtain information about exact household income, the number of cattle owned by the household may be a proxy indicator). Two general principles should be followed when defining indicators:

- *Optimal ignorance*: Knowing what is not worth knowing and prioritizing the issues to be evaluated; limiting the collection of data to answering the questions that are most relevant to understanding these issues (Chambers 1993: 18 – 19). This can be done by carefully selecting one or two questions through which crucial information can be obtained. Key questions can serve as indicators. If community members are to be involved, it is important that they choose the questions and the form and method of measurement and expression (Davis-Case 1989:25).

- *Appropriate imprecision*: Not gathering data with more accuracy than is needed to understand the priority issues for evaluation (Chambers 1993:20).

A useful indicator is:

- *Measurable*: Able to be recorded and analyzed either qualitatively or quantitatively.
- *Precise or accurate*: Defined and understood the same way by all people.
- *Consistent*: Not changing over time.
- *Sensitive*: Changing proportionally in response to actual changes in the condition or item being measured.

It is best to identify a set of indicators for measuring progress toward any goal and to identify both qualitative and quantitative measures that will reinforce each other. This will increase the rigour and relevance of the evaluation and the reliability of the results. In some cases, open-ended questions with key stakeholders will be more revealing than predefined indicators, especially for the capacity-building and empowering outcomes of participatory research. Furthermore, because one can rarely know the main issues before the project has an effect, it is sometimes not appropriate to identify indicators in advance. In any case, it is important to prioritize the issues to be evaluated and to distinguish between what is and what is not worth knowing, thus limiting the collection of data to answering the questions that are most relevant and not gathering data with more accuracy than is needed.

Other factors to consider when defining indicators:

- Develop one or more indicators for each piece of information needed.
- Different community groups and individuals will have different indicators. The choice of indicators for measuring progress, changes,

success, and failure will be influenced by perceptions of what these terms mean to the various stakeholders; therefore, the indicators used to measure them will depend on who chooses the indicators.

- Identifying indicators in a participatory way with a variety of stakeholders is a time-consuming process. Too much focus on defining indicators may sidetrack the project and consume resources and time at the expense of other, more productive activities. Depending on the purpose of the monitoring and evaluation, open-ended questions may provide sufficient information and flexibility to allow the articulation of different values and views.

- Indicators are often site - specific and seasonal. They may also be transitory and will have to be reassessed continually during a project to ensure that they are still a valid measure of the change being studied.

Exercise (from the first workshop)
The use of indicators (what?)

Translate the object (s) into clear and measurable indicators. Each object should have at least one indicator, but feel free to list more than one. Suggest for each indicator how it could be measured.

Results
See Tables 2 and 3 at the end of the chapter.

Exercise (from the second workshop)
Selecting indicators

As we already experienced during the 1st workshop, it is very difficult to identify indicators for the participatory monitoring and evaluation of project progress. Please review the following aspects or components of your project and identify two appropriate indicators for each of them. At the same time, please think about how you could measure these indicators.

Results

Component	Indicator	Tool
Social development	School enrolment of female children Income from agriculture	Secondary data analysis, and interviewing Secondary data analysis, questionnaire, interviewing
Participation and decision-making	Degree of women's satisfaction about decisions made Degree of subgroups' satisfaction about decisions made	Filming, matrix score
Communica- tion	Number of meetings Number of participants at meetings Degree to which participants know each other	Meeting records, interviewing
Capacity development	Mastering of technologies Results of new rules and regulations	Interviewing
Learning	Number of people trained Satisfaction about teaching tool used User-based learning groups	Group discussion, key informant interviewing

Reflection

This exercise helped the teams dig deeper into the complex question of indicators. The teams confessed that although this group exercise was served to sharpen definitions, there were still difficulties in producing meaningful and clear indicators for all categories. The teams concluded that further refinement was required and that more effort and time must be set aside to accomplish this.

Who? — identifying the implementers

In PM&E, the distinction between "for whom" and "who" becomes blurred, i.e., users and implementers (evaluators) are the same people. PM&E involves local people to monitor and evaluate social and environmental change. During the project cycle they can also carry out, together with the researchers, systematic monitoring and evaluation of the process (i.e., who is participating and who is being influenced directly by the research). Information from this kind of monitoring can be fed back into project design to help improve and adapt the methods and research strategy and to improve project management. This approach is known as adaptive management.

Researchers should be selective about when and how they involve local people in monitoring and evaluation, as this does not necessarily benefit the people directly and has an opportunity cost in terms of local people's time, which should not be undervalued. If local people are involved, it is important that they share the objectives of the PM&E process, that they contribute to defining indicators that are meaningful to them, and that they experience direct benefits from their involvement.

A note about external evaluators: During the project cycle, outside evaluators may provide important additional feedback on how the research can be improved. This may involve PM&E methods to capture community and special-group perspectives and to clarify issues of representation. Participatory evaluation exercises facilitated by an external evaluator in ongoing projects can combine external evaluation with training of researchers in evaluation tools and can actually be an entry point for encouraging more systematic monitoring and introducing an adaptive management approach.

Exercise (from the first workshop)
Identifying the implementers of participatory monitoring and evaluation (who?)

Please define, for each of the listed objectives and related indicator (s), who will be responsible for doing the PM&E. Be as specific as possible.

Results

See Tables 2 and 3 at the end of the chapter

Exercise（from the second workshop）
Decision-making in the PM&E process

Participation is a central feature in the PM&E process. However, there are various ways to participate with, likely, different results. Please reflect on the decision-making in your own PM&E fieldwork by filling in the following table.

Results *

Research step or activity	Who controls decision-making?	Who implements the activity?	Who will benefit from the results?
Identification of research problem	Researchers	Researchers, village members, local officials	Village members, researchers, government
Defining the research questions	Researchers, village members	Researchers	Village members, researchers
Defining the methods and selecting the tools	Researchers, village members	Village members, researchers, local officials	Village members
Implementation	Researchers, village members	Village members, researchers	Village members
Monitoring	Researchers	Village members	Village members, researchers, local officials
Evaluation	Researchers, donors	Researchers, donors	Researchers, donors

* Based on the GAAS project. The KIB case is very similar.

Reflection

This exercise served as an eye-opener to both teams. It made us realize that in both projects the research teams (still) exercised strong control over the various research cycle steps in terms of decision-making. It forced us to reflect more profoundly and systematically on what participation means and implies for the research process both conceptually and methodologically.

When? — establishing the timing

Activities can be monitored and evaluated at different stages of the project cycle, and different stakeholders may be involved at each stage. We normally distinguish three phases in a project cycle: pre-project, in-project, and post-project. At the stage of proposal development, participatory research can be assessed by examining the context (environmental, social, political) and the purpose of the project to roughly anticipate what level and scale of participation and representation is appropriate or feasible. The main issues to consider here include institutional and researcher capacity and motivation; appropriateness of the participatory method; contextual constraints and associated risks; and ethical issues.

The timing of in-project monitoring and evaluation depends on information needs. In some cases, monitoring may be ongoing and carried out at regular, predefined intervals (daily, weekly, etc.); e.g., when considering physical changes (soil quality, number of animals, etc.). Occasional simple evaluation exercises to look at project progress and intermediate outputs and outcomes before key decisions are made may help researchers and the community decide on the direction of the project or understand the direction in which the project is heading. Alternatively, regular evaluation sessions might be scheduled as part of the planning and management process. Evaluation activities may also be held in response to a special problem or crisis that the project is facing (Davis-Case 1989:40).

External, post-project evaluations are useful in establishing conceptual lessons from case studies of successful or less successful participatory research approaches for natural resource management. Learning what methods worked well or less well in each context and what did not work at all after the project has been completed provides important lessons for future research. Using qualitative and participatory evaluation methods to obtain information from the various stakeholders, including community subgroups, will enable an understanding of different perspectives on project results.

After the project has been completed for some time, evaluation can reveal the longer-term results of the research and address such questions as the resilience of behaviour and institutions initiated during the research and the sustainability of new practices (are the environmental conditions better? are people still applying the techniques?). Such longer-term evaluation might provide useful insights as certain benefits (such as improved sustainability or productivity) of participatory research for natural resource management can only be observed after a considerable period.

Exercise (from the first workshop)
The timing of PM&E in your project (when?)

Please prepare a calendar for each of the listed PM&E activities defined in the exercises carried out so far.

Results
See Tables 2 and 3 at the end of the chapter.

How? — selecting the tools

In choosing the tools for PM&E, it is crucial to reflect on what is being assessed, for whom the information is intended, the available time and resources, and, last but not least, the skills of those who will be using the tools. For example, it makes no sense to use written forms if participants cannot read; pictorial diagrams may be more appropriate.

Without going into the details of the rapidly growing number of tools that are used for PM&E (e.g., IUCN 1997; Margoluis and Salafsky 1998; Dayal, van Wijk, Mukherjee 2000) we consider that many of the PRA tools are useful. Examples are:

- community or (micro) watershed resource maps; farm maps; transect maps
- transect walks; transect plots
- historical lines; seasonal diagrams
- social maps; Venn diagrams
- ranking diagrams of various kinds
- strengths, weaknesses, opportunities, and threats (SWOT) analysis
- pictorial diagrams
- impact diagrams and matrices
- group brainstorming exercises
- focus group discussions

Use can be made of drawings, posters, photographs, theatre, role playing, or games. In addition, tools from "traditional" social science research can be adopted, such as:

- direct measurement
- direct observation
- informal conversation
- interviews of various kinds
- questionnaires
- surveys
- self-evaluation forms
- personal journals

Exercise (from the first workshop)
Selecting tools for PM&E (how?)

Please indicate which tools you know about or have heard of that are useful for doing PM&E. Return to your own project. Please identify the appropriate tool(s) for each of the identified PM&E activities in your project.

Results

See Tables 2 and 3 at the end of the chapter.

Synthesis

In this chapter we have outlined key concepts and methods used in PM&E and highlighted the interconnectedness of the six key questions and the importance of looking critically at participation as a process. Continuous, critical, and careful reflection on each of these questions and issues is required.

Exercise (from the second workshop)
Reflecting on PM&E fieldwork

Please identify, on a card, the most important thing that you learned from the PM&E presentation made by the other team. On another card, please write the one thing that you would like to learn more about.

How do your cards relate to the six key PM&E questions (i.e., the magic wheel of PM&E)?

Concerning the "still to learn more about" cards, are there topics that you consider more important than others?

Results (See next page)

Results

Question	Things learned	Things to be learned	Score*
Why?	The role and importance of PM&E The essence of PM&E	What exactly is the goal of PM&E How to select a good entry point What to do if farmers are not willing to cooperate	
For whom?	Researchers, farmers and officials	How to analyze and summarize the results How to share the results How to write a PM&E report How to extend the results to other farmers	10
What?	The need to identify indicators	How to define clear and meaningful indicators The difference between outputs and impact How to combine monitoring and evaluation	10
Who?	Researchers, farmers, and officials	How to coordinate contributions of various participants How to enhance farmers' enthusiasm during the process How to strengthen cooperation	4
How?	Choice of method Procedures and tools Use of PRA tools such as matrix, resource maps, interview Participatory technology development Sharing the work Cooperation	How to discover problems How to do self-monitoring How to combine PM&E and PTD	6
When?		When to implement the process How to use PM&E through the whole project cycle	4

* At the end of the exercise, participants voted on the two most important things to be learned.

Reflection

This exercise was a useful way to take stock at the end of the second workshop (and 1 year of fieldwork). The teams had learned many things, but also made a long list of things yet to be learned or learned more about covering five of the six questions.

Table 2. Results of exercises carried out by the GAAS project team at the first workshop.

Project research topic: Water resource management

Why conduct PM&E?

1. To identify problems, to analyze reasons, to find out solutions, and to improve project plan and implementation.
2. To find out to what extent the project research meets the needs of the local people, local government and researchers.
3. To find out to what extent the project facilitates the sustainable utilization and management of natural resources.

	Outputs	**Outcomes and impact**	**Reach**
What?	Effective management group Effective management regulations	Improved management capacity of community organization Value of and attitude toward resource use	Households within or outside the project area, local governments, local hydraulic department, project researchers and visitors
Indicators	Improved services of management staff Fairness of water distribution Increased irrigated areas (village level and household level) Effectiveness of facility operations	Timeliness of water distribution Ease of water fee collection Decreased conflicts in water distribution Labour mobilization forbuilding and maintenance of facility	No. of visitors Times of experience sharing with other researchers No. of villages that have adopted the measures of water resource management of the project
Who?	Management group Beneficial household Researchers	Local households Researchers Local government Village committee	Local households Researchers Local government Village committee

Table 2 Concluded

	Outputs	Outcomes and impact	Reach
For whom?	Local government Target community Hydraulic department Researchers	Local government Target community Researchers	Local government Target community Researchers
When?	Following the workshop, during last year of project implementation		
Tools	Matrix scoring Semi-structured interviewing at household and group levels Sampling survey Community resource mapping Self-monitoring book		

Table 3. Results of exercises carried out by the KIB project team at the first workshop.

Project research topic: capacity-building in community technology development

Why implement PM&E?

1. To improve the project (identify problems during the implementation process; improve participation; summarize experiences and lessons; identify new challenges; donors' requirement)
2. To make the project more easily accepted (win more trust; capacity-building of participants)

	Project goals				Reach
	Sustainable farmer's nursery	Learned grafting technique for fruit trees	Change of perceptions about new technology	Enhanced economic income	Community, farmers and government
Indicators	No. of nurseries No. of seedlings produced per nursery Survival rate of key species	20% people attended training (at least 1/3 females) Successful duplication after training (> 60 %)	60% farmers willing to attend training	Cost of seedlings reduced by 1/3 Project benefit more than 30% of households	Frequency of government organized training No. of outside visitors
For whom?	Farmers and researchers Individual households and researchers Project, and nursery managers	Researchers and trainers Donors and relevant farmers	Project team, decision-makers and donors	Nursery managers, farmers, and foresters Donors, project team and farmers	Donors and other projects Donors and other projects
Who do?	Farmers, researchers, and foresters Project team, and farmer representatives Nursery managers and foresters	Trainees and non-trainees Project team, forestry bureau, and representatives of trainees	Project coordinator, local officials, women leaders, teachers, and representatives of local farmers	Social foresters, nursery managers, and foresters Project team and involved villagers	Forestry bureau, village leaders, and project team Project team and village leaders

Table 3 Concluded

	Project goals				Reach
	Sustainable farmer's nursery	Learned grafting technique for fruit trees	Change of perceptions about new technology	Enhanced economic income	Community, farmers and government
What learned?	With outside assistance, farmers' nurseries can be established Experience in nursery development for other projects Methods for developing survival rate indicators for PM&E	Training is only one of many learning approaches Factors limiting farmers adoption of new technologies	Self-reliance and development is a key to community development	Advanced nursery techniques Proper selection of beneficiary is a key to project success	Participation of government is important to success One of dissemination
Potential users?	Farmers, forestry agency Other farmers within watershed, donors, extension agencies in forestry and agriculture, other project Forestry agency, nursery managers	Trainers, government, project team Forestry agency, community and farmers	Decision-makers, donors, and other projects	Forestry station, other researchers, and other nursery managers Other project managers, farmers within watershed	Project coordinating institutions, officials, and other project Other projects and government extension agencies

Table 3 Concluded

| | Project goals | | | | Reach |
	Sustainable farmer's nursery	Learned grafting technique for fruit trees	Change of perceptions about new technology	Enhanced economic income	Community, farmers and government
How to use?	Project team's supervision in the fields Transplanting, improving environment, enhancing income, learning experience, extension and achieving objectives Improving nursery technology, selecting proper key species	Improving training methods and organizing approach Larger extension	Process and approach for mobilizing community, experience learned from project design, implementation, monitoring and evaluation, effective use the project impacts	Demonstration and extension Learned experience from beneficiary	Modifying project design, more input for extension More extension
When?	During phase 2 project implementation period				
Tools	Matrix scoring, key informant interviews	Social map and semi-structured interviews	Social map, questionnaire, participatory observation	Resource flow diagram, questionnaire, participatory observation, and secondary data	Institutional diagram, key informant interview

3. "We help them, they help us": experience in Yunnan

The lively interactions about the meaning of the core PM&E concepts and questions and the active participation in the training method and process described in the previous chapters allowed the KIB and GAAS teams to apply key PM&E concepts in the field and to experiment with various tools. In this and the following two chapters, we describe and reflect on how this was done. This chapter details the KIB experience and how PM&E was slowly, but progressively integrated into the "People and Resource Dynamics in Mountainous Watersheds" project (PARDYP) in Yunnan. Chapters 4 and 5 are dedicated to the monitoring and evaluation experiences of the GAAS team in Guizhou.

PARDYP: goals and process

The goals of the PARDYP team's PM&E work, as defined during the first training workshop in Guiyang (July 1999), were:

- To improve the project for development of a second phase,
- To identify problems encountered in the project,
- To determine new issues and new needs at the project site,
- To enhance the self-development capacity of local participants,
- To meet donors' needs,
- To increase the transparency of the project and, therefore, to increase accountability,
- To increase the participation of the various stakeholders,
- To learn from experience and mistakes.

Identification of these objectives marked the beginning of a step-by-step process that we have captured below (Fig. 6). In the following sections, we present the

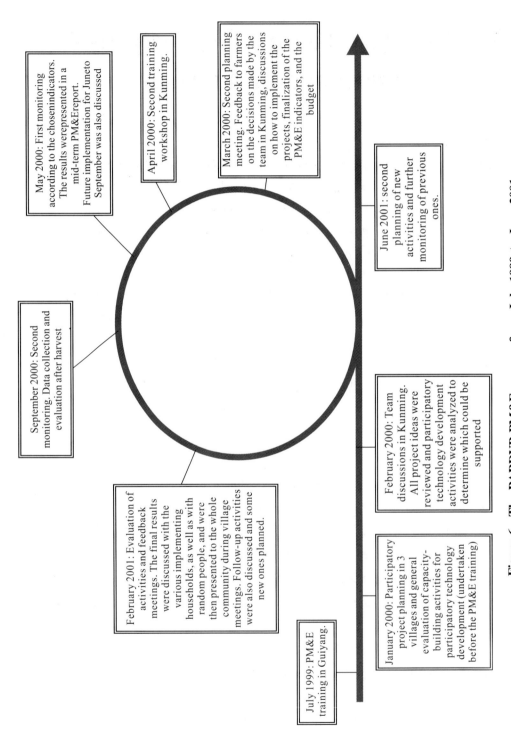

Figure 6. The PARDYP PM&E process from July 1999 to June 2001

May 2000: First monitoring according to the chosen indicators. The results were presented in a mid-term PM&E report. Future implementation for June to September was also discussed

April 2000: Second training workshop in Kunming.

March 2000: Second planning meeting. Feedback to farmers on the decisions made by the team in Kunming, discussions on how to implement the projects, finalization of the PM&E indicators, and the budget

September 2000: Second monitoring. Data collection and evaluation after harvest

June 2001: second planning of new activities and further monitoring of previous ones.

February 2001: Evaluation of activities and feedback meetings. The final results were discussed with the various implementing households, as well as with random people, and were then presented to the whole community during village meetings. Follow-up activities were also discussed and some new ones planned.

February 2000: Team discussions in Kunming. All project ideas were reviewed and participatory technology development activities were analyzed to determine which could be supported

July 1999: PM&E training in Guiyang.

January 2000: Participatory project planning in 3 villages and general evaluation of capacity-building activities for participatory technology development (undertaken before the PM&E training)

details and milestones of the planning, execution, and reflection that were carried out at the various stages so far. As illustrated in the figure (see also Figure 2 in chapter 1), this process has not been linear. Before doing so, we introduce the participants in the process.

The participants

The following people and groups have been involved in the fieldwork at various levels.

At the county level (Baoshan)

- Two officials from the forestry bureau have been involved in the planning, implementation, and monitoring of the rehabilitation and community forestry projects. They provide technical training to local people and were trained in participatory rural appraisal (PRA).
- Five officials from the hydrology bureau have been involved in the planning, establishment, and monitoring of the erosion plots and hydrological stations. They regularly train farmers in how to collect and monitor the hydrological data and the erosion plots data, which they then analyze. Several were trained in PRA and PM&E, and in water and sediment analysis methods (in Nepal).
- One person from the agricultural bureau gives advice on and provides local seed varieties.
- The land bureau provides secondary data for our research.
- The meteorological bureau provided technical support for the establishment of a meteorological station and helps process and analyze the data collected there.

At the township level

- One person from the forestry station has been involved in the project and cooperates with the forestry bureau in all of its activities.

At the village level

- Officials coordinate activities and take part in the planning and monitoring. They are the main providers of information about the various villages. As they are the local coordinators, it is particularly important to build relations of trust with them, if any activity is to take place.

At the community level

- The village leaders act as coordinators at the village level and take part in the planning and monitoring of activities.
- Farmers, both women and men, plan and implement community development activities and help monitor the activities carried out at the field stations. At the beginning, they only implemented some of the rehabilitation and the community forestry activities, but now they are also involved in the planning stages.

The PARDYP team

- Xu Jianchu is the project coordinator; Yang Lixin, Qian Jie, and Stephanie Mas are responsible for the forestry, rehabilitation, and community development activities; Gao Fu for the watershed dynamics studies; Wang Yuhua for geographic information system (GIS) activities; and Ji Yunheng for researching biopesticides.
- Other members of the Department of Ethnobotany sometimes participate in specific research activities.

Work in the field: activities and outcomes

The PM&E activities can be divided into four parts (apart from the training process described earlier):

1. Participatory project planning using PRA, participatory technology development (PTD), and PM&E methods and tools
2. Monitoring and evaluation of activities
3. Feedback meetings with local people
4. Planning of new activities

Participatory project planning

In January 2000, the project team made its first PM&E field trip. Gao Fu (watershed dynamics studies), Qian Jie (the forestry, rehabilitation, and community development activities), Xu Jianchu (project coordinator), Wang Jianhua (ethnobotanist), Yang Zhiwei (botanist), Ma Xing (Baoshan Hydrology Bureau), and Zhao Mingshou (Baoshan Forestry Bureau) carried out PTD activities in three villages: Damaidi, Yangjia and Xizhuang (see Fig. 7).

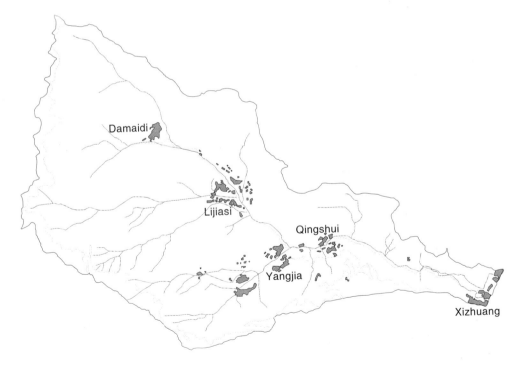

Figure 7. Map of the Xizhuang watershed

In each village, the PTD activities were scheduled according to the following six steps:

- 1. Getting started: the goals of the first step are to broaden the understanding among all the stakeholders involved (technicians, farmers, researchers) of the local situation in terms of socio-economic, cultural and political dimensions, and to agree about next steps in the process that will benefit the villagers. The PTD practitioners carried out the following tasks: selecting the area, introducing themselves to the villagers, building trust, ana-lyzing the natural resource management practices and problems, and establishing a basis for cooperation with the community, group(s) of families and indigenous/ local specialists. The tools used were a community walk and transect map, agro-ecosystems and social conditions maps, participant observation (of indigenous/local knowledge and customs), and identification of indigenous/local specialists (for each of the different agro-ecosystems).

- 2. Looking for things to try (innovations): the goal is to learn about indigenous/ local knowledge and its contribution to joint analysis, problem ranking, and formulation of potential solutions (innovations). The PTD practitioners together with the local people identified the sources of indigenous/local knowledge (specialists, innovators, experienced farmers, healers, forest users) and "outside" sources of knowledge. The tools used were diagrams drawn by specialists (depicting natural and social timelines or cycles, landuse histories, village history) and workshops.

- 3. Designing experiments: the goal is to design experiments and innovations that respond to farmers' interests and needs, strengthen their (management, organizational and experimental) knowledge, skills and practices, and improve their quality of life/livelihood. The PTD practitioners together with farmers reviewed existing capacities and practices of experimentation, and planned and designed selected experiments to be implemented by farmers and/or indigenous/local specialists. Tools used were participatory technology analysis and a (experiment) design workshop.

- 4. Trying out innovations: the goal of this important step is to implement innovations/experiments and in doing so build or strengthen farmers' skills to manage, monitor and document the process. The PTD practitioners supported and facilitated farmer group building, exchange among farmers, and process documentation (achievements, failures, modifications). The main tool used was the regular group meeting.

- 5. Sharing the results: the goals are to exchange experiences and communicate results (ideas, principles, techniques) to other experimenters, neighbors, scientists or visitors from abroad. PTD practitioners supported the mobilization of farmer experimenter networks, reporting of results, diffusion of results; and tools used included farmer-to-farmer training, technology competitions study tours and farmer self-evaluation.

- 6. Keeping up the process: the goal of the final step is to create favorable conditions for ongoing experimentation and sustainable natural resource management. PTD practitioners contribute to the consolidation of processes such as group organization, inter-village networking and cooperation, and linking farmers and specialists. Tools used include participatory impact monitoring, organizational development techniques, and networking techniques.

As a part of this process small grant projects were designed with volunteer farmers, detailed information was collected about their households, and monitoring and evaluation indicators were identified. In particular, the following questions guided the process:
- What do you want to do with this small grant?
- Why do you want to do it?
- What kind of support do you need, such as material, financial, and technical assistance?

– Who will carry out the activities in your family?

– When do you want to begin your project?

– How can we monitor the project and evaluate its success or failure?

– Who will/can monitor and evaluate activities during the project?

In February, the team discussed the results of the trip. We reviewed the field reports and discussed the cost and feasibility of each small grant according to the household action plans. We also discussed the technical support role of the Baoshan Forestry Bureau staff in the participatory technology development process.

In March, the second project planning stage began. Qian Jie and Zhao Mingshou visited individual households in the villages to review their action plans for on-farm experiments, make final decisions about implementation of activities, and discuss the schedule and responsibilities for monitoring and evaluation. Eventually, for each small grant project, the action plans were approved by the project team and these served as contracts with the local farmers. We now turn our attention to what happened in the 3 villages.

Damaidi village: Damaidi belongs to Lijiasi administrative village and is located in the upper reaches of Xizhuang watershed. It has about 90 households with 430 people and one primary school with three teachers and 60 pupils.

The total land area is about 231 mu (15.4 ha; 1 mu = 0.066 ha or 1 ha = 15 mu) and the average amount of farmland per person is only 0.54 mu. The major crops are corn and wheat. Due to low fertility and lack of water for irrigation, productivity is low: only 150 kg/mu for corn and 100 kg/mu for wheat. Households have a total of 50 mu of tea gardens where old tea species have been grown for more than 30 years. This kind of tea has a low yield and is of low quality. Farmers themselves process the tea leaves, then sell them to a middleman in the Banqiao and Shaba town markets. The price is always around RMB ¥ 8 – 10/kg (1 United States dollar [USD] = 8.27 Renminbi [RMB]). They also have 73 mu of land with more than 4 000 wild walnut trees.

The community meeting was held at the village leader's house. At first, eight farmers attended, then others joined in. Four groups of two people were formed for the PRA exercises; matrix scoring and ranking focused on livestock (Table 4).

The main issues and possible projects mentioned involved tea production, fruit production, and livestock. Although tea was an important source of cash income, production costs were high, as farmers had to purchase chemical fertilizers and pesticides. At the same time, the quality of the tea produced was low. The farmers wanted to experiment with new species, but these are expensive when purchased from the government extension stations. They also wanted training in tree grafting techniques (for grafting wild walnut and other fruit trees) and in how to improve the management of orchards.

Four people volunteered to implement livestock development and tea nursery projects. Suggestions included the introduction of a new species of goat and the building of pig sheds. Training in grafting techniques was also suggested (see Table 4). The team mentioned that it had limited funds and would contribute mainly in terms of technical support; we pointed out that the farmers themselves should initiate the activities.

The project team discussed the mistakes that we thought we had made, what had been omitted, and how we could improve our use of PRA tools. It was suggested that the social map include a "wealth" classification. In addition, it was recommended that the transect walk include the altitude of each land use form, and historical comments, such as land use changes and the policies determining them, land tenure changes, etc. The team discussed the feasibility of the activities suggested by farmers and how to improve the benefit-sharing arrangements. We realized that the farmers who had come to the meeting were either relatives or friends of the village leader. It was suggested, for example, that Qian Jie, who would be in charge of community development activities, approach members of the PRA network for advice on management styles for livestock development.

The projects approved after the team discussions were: building pig sheds, training in grafting of walnut trees, development of a tea nursery, and the introduction of new goat species.

Table 4. Results of matrix scoring and ranking of livestock with four households in Damaidi village

Live-stock	As helper	Market value	Provide manure	Good taste for food	Low cost (labour and fodder)	Disease resistance	Easy breeding and growth	Total
Goat		* * * * *	* * * * *		* * * * *	* * * * *	* * * * *	25
Cattle	* * * * *	* * * *	* * *		* * * *	* * * *		20
Buffalo	* * * * *	* * * *	* * *		* * *	* * * *		19
Pig		* * * *	* * * *	* * * * *		* *	* * *	18
Horse	* * * * *	* * * *	* *		* * *			14
Poultry		* * * *		* * * * *	* *		* * *	14
Dog	* * * * *							5

Note: All farmers thought goat meat tasted best, but they did not consume it themselves due to its high market value.

Yangjia village: Yangjia belongs to Qingshui administrative village. Located at about the middle of the Xizhuang watershed, it has 56 households with a total of 236 people. There are two primary schools nearby, in Qingshui and in Langmaidi. Livestock includes buffalo and pigs, with an average of one or two per household. Most of the men take outside jobs during off-seasons.

According to the wealth criteria developed by the farmers, 16 households (30.8%) are rich, 27 (51.9%) are considered "ordinary," and 9 (17.3%) are poor (Table 5).

Farmers have access to about 135 mu (9 ha) of farmland at an average of 0.57 mu per person. Due to better and more informed management, crop yields in Yangjia are higher than in other communities: 300 kg/mu for corn and 200 kg/mu for wheat. Tea gardens occupy about 120 mu, and farmers put a lot of effort into managing them. Tea is the main source of income and productivity is high. Local farmers are known for being good tea producers. They are currently planning to plant new species on 300 mu of swidden. Local forest resources are also abundant because villagers follow strict regulations for the management of their communal forests.

Table 5. Local criteria for ranking wealth in Yangjia

Rich household	Ordinary household	Poor household
Has savings Produces enough food by farming Has more livestock and poultry All family members are healthy Makes money through off-farm employment Can build new house	Has no debt Needs to buy rice from the outside market	Has debts Has bad land with landslides Has less livestock Has sick or handicapped family member(s) Has more tuition burden Members don't want to work hard Has unlucky marriage Has naughty children

In Yangjia, most villagers had been informed of the meeting, but only 12 to 15 attended. Four groups of three people were formed. The same PRA tools were used as in Damaidi, but a historical diagram of the main environmental changes in the village from the 1950s to the 1990s (natural disasters, crop species, fertilizers and pesticides used, forest cover, and farming technologies used) was added. Indeed, landslides and finding ways to control them were previously identified as a main issue in Yangjia. Scoring and ranking thus focused on fruit tree and bamboo species (Table 6). In the afternoon, many project ideas were put forward, but at first no one wanted to volunteer to carry them out.

Several main issues and proposals emerged. Soil fertility had to be improved to offset the increased population and associated reduction in the amount of land available per household. The problem of landslides was discussed, as well as the need to improve tea and corn yields to have more to sell or exchange for rice.

Project ideas included introducing soybeans as a new crop. Farmers thought soybeans would be suitable for the local climate and would also improve soil fertility. The team promised to try to get more information about suitable species. Tea and walnut nurseries were also recommended, as well as "fruit" or sweet corn. Farmers had grown corn only for fodder, not as a food crop, but they had heard ofa species that humans could eat and wanted to try it.

Table 6. Results of matrix scoring and ranking of fruit trees with six farmers from different households in Yangjia.

Fruit tree	Good taste	Easy to sell	High productivity	Less land occupation	High market price	Total
Little apple	* * * *	* * * *	* * * * *	* * * * *	* * * *	22
Walnut	* * * * *	* * * * *	* * * * *	*	* * * * *	21
Peach	* * * * *	* * *	* * * *	* * * *	* * *	19
Persimmon	* *	* * * * *	* * * * *	* *	* * * * *	19
Plum	* * *	* *	* * * * *	* * * * *	* *	17
Pear	* * * * *	* *	* *	* *	* *	13
Apple	* * * * *	*	* *	* * * *	*	13

Finally, they also wanted to plant bamboo to control erosion and stop landslides. However, they pointed out that this would not be possible because the lands where landslides occur were in private hands, belonging to three or four households. The owners were willing to exchange this land for communal property to make the project possible, but the other farmers would not agree to trade good communal farmland for land that was degraded. For the private landowners, planting bamboo was out of the question at that time, because even though the land was degraded, it still had to be used to produce wheat and corn. Planting bamboo would interfere with these crops.

At first no one volunteered to carry out any of these projects. Everyone wanted them to be carried out on communal land so that everyone would share the benefits and no one would risk their own land. Lengthy discussions followed in which the project team explained that this was not really acceptable. Eventually, it was decided that tea and walnut nurseries could be established on communal land, while the village leader and another farmer would carry out soybean and corn experiments on their own land. For the bamboo project, each farmer would plant trees and the team would then pay them RMB ¥ 2.5 for each tree that survived.

The projects that were approved after the team meetings were: an on-farm experiment with new corn varieties, an on-farm experiment with soybeans, and establishment of tea and walnut nurseries.

Xizhuang village: Xizhuang belongs to Wofu administrative village. It is located in the downstream portion of the Xizhuang watershed and has 105 households with a population of 410 people. It has several primary and high schools. Most (80%) of the men engage in off-farm employment and the living standard is better than in the other two villages.

Villagers have paddy fields with high productivity, as well as old tea gardens planted in 1959, which are less productive. Because there are no forests within the area, farmers must buy firewood for daily use in the market. A cement factory nearby causes air pollution.

The process in Xizhuang presented some new challenges. The team arrived early in the morning, and waited a long time for the villagers to meet, but no one came. When we approached the households directly, farmers said that their leader had not informed them about the meeting. In fact, the project team had had some conflict with this village leader in the past. In the end, we carried out the various PRA exercises in individual households and asked farmers to come to the public place in the afternoon. To our disappointment, only two people came.

The projects suggested by the two people who attended the afternoon meeting were the development of village wastelands and the planting of several fruit trees. However, the farmer interested in fruit trees later withdrew because he thought the team was lying about providing support and would later ask for money; he tried to convince the other farmer to leave as well. The wasteland management project was approved after team discussions.

Monitoring and evaluation of activities

The following community PTD activities were evaluated through interviews with farmers according to the framework established by the PARDYP team during the first training workshop in Kunming (see chapter 2, Table 3).

Nursery development: Most farmers considered the establishment of the nursery for high-quality tea species in Lijiasi (Damaidi) successful. The official who implemented the project mastered the skills necessary for nursery development, and the survival rate of the plants was high (over 85%) due to good management, despite many problems caused by the cold weather in 1999. All the tea seedlings were sold to villagers at a low price, and the nursery provided cuttings for the other farmers.

On the other hand, the walnut nursery in Qingshui (Yangjia) was considered unsuccessful due to poor management and a failure to share the benefits. Problems identified by the farmers were:

- The project had been negotiated only with local officials, who then submitted it to someone else. No contract was established to determine the responsibilities of the various stakeholders, so when conflicts arose, the local officials did nothing.
- The project workers lacked background information about the community. The local farmer was incapable of implementing the project, so no one was surprised at the low growth and survival rates.
- No monitoring and evaluation system had been established. Even though the PARDYP team paid a salary and allowance to the farmer, he sold the walnut seedlings and pocketed the money.

Establishment of a pear orchard: The PARDYP team provided good-quality pear seedlings to Yangjia village at no cost. Villagers planted them on both private and communal land. The trees grew well on the private property (survival rate over 95%), but most of the trees on communal land were stolen by other farmers.

Regarding the pear variety, the following advantages and disadvantages were noted by farmers (no breakdown by sex):

Advantages	Disadvantages
• Growth rate was excellent; trees produced fruit in 3 years. • The pear trees could be intercropped with soybean and squash, thus solving the problem of more people/less farmland. • The necessary management skills are not complicated; management does not require more time or labour.	• The PARDYP team did not provide enough information about the pear species. Farmers said they did not know anything about taste and other characteristics. • Villagers also lacked market information. Although they were eager to plant many trees, they were uncertain what the demand would be in 3 years.

Training in grafting and pruning: Many farmers found this kind of training necessary. The skills are simple, easy to learn, and are of great benefit. However, they complained that the selection of trainees was not made public; few people knew who had been trained, so the techniques were not passed along to others. It became clear that keeping up the process through farmer-to-farmer training and networking is key to sustaining PTD activities.

Livelihood development experiments implemented in 2000 were also monitored through farmer interviews, according to the criteria and indicators established by the farmers during the planning stage (see Table 7).

Table 7. **Example of an information chart prepared by farmers during the project planning phase**

Item	Information collected
Stakeholder	Ms. WS, female, 31 years old
Household	Husband, 33 years old; stepmother, 60 years old; son, 5 years old; daughter, 10 years old
Land use	2 mu of dry land, 4 mu tea garden, 0.07 mu home garden, which can be modified as tea nursery
Livestock	2 pigs, 3 buffaloes, 7chickens
Income	From selling tea (usually 50 kg), RMB ¥ 500; selling pigs, RMB ¥ 1 500; selling chickens, RMB ¥ 100; off-farm employment, RMB ¥ 2 000

Table 7 concluded

Item	Information collected
Expenses	Rice, RMB ¥ 1 000; fodder, RMB ¥ 200; school tuition, RMB ¥ 500 – 600; maintenance, RMB ¥ 500 – 600
What?	Establish nursery stock of new tea species
Why?	New tea species has high yield and higher market prices. The nursery stock can help improve local people's tea gardens in the future.
What do you need?	Materials: tea branches, pesticide, long plastic pipes; labour: preparation of land by farmers; technical support: transplanting, nursery management
Who?	Ms. WS and her husband
When to start?	Transplanting should take place in June 2000
Evaluation indicators	Survival rate of tea seedlings; the number of seedlings bought in the community; the price of tea seedlings (should be lower than the market price)
Who will monitor?	Local coordinator and officials

Note: 1 mu = 0.066 ha or 666 m^2.1 United States dollar (USD) = 8.27 Renminbi yuan (RMB ¥). The total budget of RMB ¥ 1 220 consisted of RMB ¥ 800 for tea branches and RMB ¥ 420 for other materials.

Livestock : To start a "passing the gift project," three households were selected in Damaidi village and their purchase of seven goats was subsidized. The plan was for the first household to care for the goats for 2 years; at that point the second household would select seven goats from the group and raise them for 2 years; then the third household would choose goats. After 6 years, officials from Lijiasi administrative village would select seven goats from the third household and distribute them in a new village to replicate the project. In the first year, the number of goats had already increased to 11.

The project team decided to adopt this type of project following their experience at the planning meeting, where they realized that all the farmers who attended were either relatives or friends of the village leader. The team wanted to find a way to keep from helping only a select (and likely elite) group and extending the benefits to other people.

It is important to plan small grant projects in detail. Farmers, together with field staff, should try to think of all the issues that will arise and the support they will need during the implementation stage and include them in the funding. Once the budget has been approved, the coordinator should be strict about not providing any extra funds. In the project in Damaidi, for example, "extra" money was included in the budget for buying medicine. This is important, as farmers usually ask for more and more money during project implementation.

A second project involved pigs. Pigs are traditionally kept under the houses in a space that is difficult to clean and where disease spreads easily. One household in Damaidi was assisted to build pig sheds to improve hygiene and control diseases. Previously, this household had been able to raise six pigs a year; with the pig sheds, it can produce more than ten.

Wasteland development: One farmer in Xizhuang village volunteered to carry out on-farm experiments in wasteland development. He was given a small fund to build a house close to the land, 2 km from the village. He was trained in walnut nursery development and fruit tree production, then provided with free walnut, corn, pear, plum, and grape seedlings, which he planted. He also raised 30 rabbits, five hives of honeybees, a donkey, and 10 goats. In addition, he dug a pond, which produced more than 50 kg of fish.

This experience showed us how diverse farmers' ideas can be when it comes to increasing their household income. In this case, diversification reduced the risk that the household was facing by depending on only one main farming activity.

Demonstration of new crops: Assistance was provided to one household in Yangjia to plant soybeans on 1 mu of land with low productivity to reestablish the balance of soil nutrients and to compare this crop with the corn and tea originally planted, in terms of social, economic, and ecological benefits. Growing soybeans appeared to require less labour and time and to reduce soil pollution, as it only requires small amounts of fertilizer; it also increases soil fertility (see Table 8). Soybeans can also be traded for more rice: 1 kg of soybeans can be exchanged for 1 kg of rice, whereas 2 kg of corn are needed for 1 kg of rice. Corn is necessary to provide fodder for pigs, but brings no direct economic returns; tea brings economic benefits, but growing it is labour intensive, especially for women. Moreover, the price of tea has dropped this year, as potential purchasers on the international market now know that local farmers use a dangerous pesticide forbidden by the agricultural bureau. (Research is being carried out to develop remedy this situation.)

After this experiment, farmers decided to extend the area planted with soybeans to 50 mu. The PARDYP team provided them with 250 kg of seeds this year (February 2001).

Table 8. Economic comparison of crops grown in Yangjia

Crop	Labour input	Capital input (RMB ¥/mu)	Average yield (kg/mu)	Market price (RMB ¥/kg)	Income (RMB ¥/mu)
Soybeans var.661	Medium (simple management)	Low(average < 40, including seeds)	120	2.40	288
Soybeans var.028	Medium (simple management)	High (more than 150, seeds are expensive)	180	2.40	432
Corn	High (fertilizing, weeding, etc.)	High (average 70)	100	0.76	76
Tea	High (applying pesticides, collecting tea leaves)	High (average > 100)	50	8	400

One species of high-yield corn (Dianfeng #4) and three species of sweet corn, which can be sold at a high price, were introduced in Yangjia. With Dianfeng #4, production increased from 300 kg/mu to 525 kg/mu. This variety cannot be used for fodder, as the skin is too thick. However, it can be exchanged for rice, which cannot be planted in the uplands and thus has to be purchased by farmers. Sweet corn varieties, on the other hand, did not grow well in the uplands, because of the low temperature and strong winds. It seems that a combination of the new variety of high-yield corn on good land and soybeans on the low-productivity lands will give the farmers sufficient resources to purchase the rice they need.

Nursery development: In June, eight farmers were trained in tea nursery establishment: six from Damaidi and two from Yangjia. In July, two tea gardens were established with different management systems. In Damaidi, the nursery is managed by one household, which will sell plants to the other villagers. They planted 27 000 seeds this year with a survival rate of 95%. In Yangjia, the community owns the nursery. One farmer was hired to manage it and he gets a salary of 2000 RMB a year. The villagers, who will share the plants, planted about 60 000 seeds. However, most of them did not participate in the training and did not plant the seeds carefully. The nursery was also badly managed; at one point, the field was not watered for 4 days. Thus, survival rate was low, at only 70%.

This project made the team realize that it is better to start small, at the individual household level, then move to a larger scale if it is successful. Large-scale activities are much harder to manage. Moreover, when farmers themselves take risks, they are more careful and more likely to be successful. If they have nothing to lose, they also have little to gain.

Two walnut nurseries were established in May, following the training of seven farmers in Yangjia and Xizhuang. Overall, the survival rate is 95%, and 400 plants are now available for planting in the upland gardens.

Training in grafting and other agricultural techniques: For 3 days in February, seven farmers in Damaidi were trained and provided with knives, wax, thread, plastic film, twine, whetstones, and walnut branches. A total of 2 500 walnut trees were grafted with a new species. The two technicians from the local forestry bureau, who trained the farmers, were expecting a survival rate of 60%, but the actual rate was only 40%. However, the farmers appreciated the training and felt confident about their newly acquired skills. Although the results of the grafting experiments on communal land were poor, survival rate was high in villagers' home gardens, and they have used their new skills to graft peach and pear trees as well. They were eager to try again next year and to organize farmer-to-farmer training.

Although this project appeared to be a failure, the farmers actually viewed it as very successful. They were not concerned about the low survival rate, but helped the team determine why it was low and how to improve it for the next time.

In June, two farmers from each village (Damaidi, Yangjia, and Xizhuang) and their village leaders visited the Baoshan tea extension station and the exhibition of new agricultural technologies. They were particularly interested in tea nurseries, tea species, and planting techniques. However, no women became involved in the activity, making the team aware that they needed to pay more attention to women's roles and relationships (with men and with other women), interests, and constraints. Increasing understanding of gender roles and relationships is equally important for project members, local partners, and local community members.

Feedback meetings

The third element in the cycle consisted of the very important feedback meetings. Returning to the villages, the team interviewed participating and nonparticipating household members, both women and men. The overall objectives of this step were:

- To find out, through direct interviews with the farmers, how much they knew about the project, what they thought about the various activities, and what kind of new activities they would be interested in developing
- To present, during village meetings, the overall goal of the project, explain how it was organized and why, and present all the activities and results in a holistic way and get feedback from farmers
- To introduce the project style and approach and the concept of self-development
- To plan for the extension of the soybean project in Yangjia and of the peach tree project in Damaidi and Yangjia

The schedule was:

- 24 *February*, *Damaidi village*: Interview farmers during the day; conduct feedback meeting at the school in the evening
- 25 *February*, *Yangjia village*: Household interviews in the afternoon; meeting to plan peach tree and soybean extension projects in the evening
- 26 *February*, *Yangjia village*: Household interviews during the day; first feedback meeting and discussions in the evening
- 27 *February*, *Yangjia and Damaidi*: Second feedback meeting in Yangjia in morning; meeting to plan peach tree project in Damaidi in the afternoon

The team carried out semi-structured interviews and sometimes open discussions with both participating and non-participating villagers. With those who had taken part in the projects, they focused on evaluation of the various activities. In addition, randomly selected households, who were not directly participating in the projects, were also asked the following questions:

- What had they heard about the project?
- Which activities did they think were the most appropriate in their context and what activities did they prefer?
- Which activities had they taken part in and what role did they play?
- What suggestions did they have for improving activities to benefit more people?
- What kinds of activities would they like to develop in the future?
- What did they think about the project?
- What kinds of activities helped people become richer in their village and in nearby villages?
- Other more specific questions, depending on who was being interviewed, concerning their interests, specialization, etc.

Evaluation of project activities by participants: The building of pig sheds was considered successful. Being able to raise more pigs significantly increased household income, but also the work burden of family members, especially the women, as they were responsible for preparing fodder. This activity includes finding green fodder, chopping it up, cooking it, and feeding it to the pigs. Having to prepare nearly twice as much fodder as previously meant that the women in the participating household had considerably less time for other activities. They were thinking about purchasing an electric grinding machine, and wanted the PARDYP team to provide a small loan for this purpose. The team had to refuse, because we only disbursed additional money for small grants projects when absolutely necessary; but the team took the opportunity to suggest that they organize as a group to share the costs. They could then charge user fees to other farmers outside the group, who would like to use the machine.

The "passing the gift" project was still successful, and the number of new breeds of goats was increasing to the point where some could be passed to the next household sooner than expected.

Many farmers were very satisfied with the tea nursery initiative. All of the tea plants from the Damaidi nursery were on order, sometimes by farmers from distant villages. The survival rate remained high.

In Yangjia, however, the project was already deemed to have failed. In February, the plants were under cover, so it was impossible to determine the exact survival rate, but the farmer who managed the nursery and forestry bureau staff expected it to be less than 50%. According to the nursery manager, this was due to several factors. First, the cuttings were done by about 20 people, very inconsistently, so that when another group of 14 people came to plant them, they had to plant some deep and some shallow, and ended up not taking sufficient care over the work. Second, after planting, the cuttings should have been shaded, but there was no funding for this, and none of the farmers had enough interest to invest in the project. Finally, after only a month, the manager quit and the field was left unwatered for about 4 days until someone was found to replace him. This management issue was discussed in depth with the villagers, who had wanted to plant the peach trees on communal land. Eventually, they decided to plant them instead on upland fields with the different farmers managing their own plots.

During the February field trip, the PARDYP team planned for the extension of the soybean crops to 50 mu. This involved about 38 households, each planting 2.5 – 10 kg of seeds. The seeds were distributed in April 2001, but no monitoring and evaluation indicators have been established so far. This will be done during the next field trip.

The establishment of new corn varieties was a failure. Although the high-yield corn grew very well, farmers reported that the local extension station wanted to introduce another variety, which they prefer. It tastes better, is easier to obtain, and although the productivity is not as high as the variety from our project, it is acceptable.

For the other activities, the results and evaluations were unchanged.

Comments from non-participating households: Most of the non-participants interviewed did not know about PARDYP. However, when asked about the various activities, they were aware of them, but surprised that they were all part of the same project. The team thus spent quite some time explaining the project and introducing themselves. Most people thought the activities were good and wanted to take part in them.

In Damaidi, a woman had tried to introduce new tea cuttings, but most of them died, possibly due to a poor use of fertilizers, she suggested. Thus, when the plants from the tea nursery projects are sold, a new training session on tea planting should be organized. In Yangjia, the village leader wanted to establish a nursery for nut trees, as nuts can be stored more easily than fruit and are also easy to sell.

In both Yangjia and Lijiasi, some farmers wanted to establish nurseries for propagating a wild vegetable called *cilabao* (local name). This species has been traditionally used in the watershed for fencing and eating (household consumption), but it also has high market value. During the field trip, a propagation project was planned by Yang Lixin and two farmers, one from Yangjia and the other from Lijiasi. Both farmers were trained to take cuttings from roots. They will be paid to acquire the cuttings from existing trees around the village and plant them on small experimental plots (about 0.3 mu in Yangjia and 0.5 mu in Lijiasi). Later this year, they will be trained further in management techniques and, if the activity is successful, farmer-to-farmer training will be organized to scale-up the project.

Several farmers in Damaidi were also interested in applying for small loans from the project; for example, to buy a grinding machine to make flour or to prepare fodder. In Ganwenkeng, a group of women would like to buy a machine to make *toufu*. These kinds of projects could become part of a micro-credit project, which could eventually be sustained by village funds. A few years ago, for example, Yangjia was given about RMB ¥ 100 000 by the government, in compensation for a road built on its land. Damaidi also received funds, but no one seems to know what happened to them. This village has no leader, because no one wants to account for the lost funds (which might have left the village together with the previous leader). The idea of a micro-credit project might motivate the farmers to look into this issue and try to solve it.

Other discussions during the field visit touched on the general development situation in the various villages and on the most significant changes that have contributed to the improvement in the standard of living. In Yangjia, the team had lengthy discussions about the various laws governing access to forest products.

In Damaidi, a project had been initiated by Gao Fu to overcome the shortage of water for irrigation during the dry season (winter); this had been identified as one of the main issues of concern during PRA exercises in 1998. In September 1999, interviews had been conducted with farmers in Damaidi and in January and August 2000, planning meetings had taken place. At first, farmers decided to build 30 small individual tanks ($1.5 - 4.5m^3$) next to their farmlands. Monitoring and evaluation indicators that were established included increased yield and more time available for other work. A local committee was established for planning, building and managing the water conservation system. It included four people elected by the villagers and a local official. In November, farmers finished building 34 tanks and asked PARDYP to support them to build another large pool ($90m^3$). The PARDYP team said that it would be able to contribute only a very small amount of money. However, farmers started construction and the tank was completed in December 2000. During the team's field trip in February, the leader of the Lijiasi administrative village said that it had still not been paid for. The team did not discuss the issue then, as we did not know enough about the project and knew that Gao Fu would evaluate it in April.

Village feedback meeting in Damaidi: The team planned a five-step process for the meeting:

- Step 1: Explain the project in its broader context, i.e., cooperation with other countries and the fact that what is learned in this village might help poor people elsewhere and contribute to raising the standard of living. The team hoped that this would motivate the villagers. We wanted to introduce the KIB and ourselves, and our project style and methods, and to highlight that the team wanted to learn from the villagers, share ideas, and provide support for their self-development and reflection on their own activities.

- Step 2: Using posters, present all project activities for the year, including the research activities, so that the villagers would understand the whole process and the project's logic. At the end of the presentation, we intended to ask if there were other activities that the villagers would be interested in.

- Step 3: Facilitate group discussions. At first, we thought we would ask three questions: What is the activity good for? Who is benefiting? and What else/other kind of support do they need for the activity? But on further reflection, we decided on only two: What benefits does it bring? and Who is benefiting? At the end of the discussion, we would ask what kinds of activities the villagers would like to add.

- Step 4: Present the results of the discussions and rank activities, including the newly proposed ones, by asking people to move to the poster representing their preferred activity. The team planned to ask women to decide first to allow them freer choice. We would then remove the poster with the largest number of votes and repeat the process for other activities.

- Step 5: Use the method described in step 4 to rank the activities the villagers would like to take part in.

The actual process contained a couple of surprises. The discussion using the posters was easy to follow and everyone looked very interested. Five groups of six or seven people were formed and given nine sheets of paper. The team asked each group to answer the first question only (What benefits does it bring?), using one sheet for each activity and drawing the activity symbol on the top. The results are presented below (Table 9).

Most of the groups of men discussed only the activities they were interested in, whereas women followed the whole process trying to discuss all alternatives. It was difficult to facilitate the meeting, as there were only two facilitators for the five groups (Qian Jie, who moved from one group to another, and Xiao Li). Thus, the process was "a little messy," but quite productive. The meeting started late (between 8 and 8:30 p. m.) and lasted a long time, as people had many questions after the group discussions. In the end, the team was unable to carry out all the planned steps, although it seems that all the people who attended the meeting (about 35) now had a good understanding of the whole project and the links between the various activities. The discussions were lively, and people agreed that this kind of meeting was excellent: "We help them, they help us."

The other positive outcome was that more and more people trusted the project team and wanted to take part in the various activities. Only relatives of the village leader had attended the previous year's meeting, so only a select few villagers had benefited from the first year's activities. (The team was told later that other people had been informed of the meeting, but did not attend because they were not interested and did not believe what they were told about the project. They thought the team was like the usual business people who come to their village and try to trick them. A few years before, a man had trained them in walnut grafting, given them branches, then asked for a percentage of the production.)

· 80 ·

Table 9: Benefits of nine small projects in Damaidi, identified by groups of villagers

New corn varieties (2)*	Tea nursery (2)	New goat species (5)
• high yield • can exchange for rice • makes wine • fodder • food • income generation • diversify of crops	• income generation • high yield • easy to collect • conserves water • new skills • drink • provides good cuttings for the community • high survival rate	• income generation • appropriate for development in mountainous areas • people already have the skills • provides fertilizer • produces a new species • food • benefits several people due to "passing the gift" • someone thought there are other species, better adapted to the cold weather
Soybean crops (3)	**Reforestation (3)**	**Peach trees (5)**
• can be intercropped with other higher plants; intensification • income generation • food • bean curd • good for crop diversification • can be exchanged for other food	• good for water • firewood • building materials for houses • timber for selling • benefits everybody • prevents floods • erosion control	• income generation • provides branches for grafting • leading to benefits for whole community • food
Pig sheds (2)	**Training (1)**	**Hydrology (2)**
• income generation • fertilizer leading to good harvest • only benefits the people who have one	• new skills/ knowledge	• controls drought; increases production and income generation • water tanks: increase productivity and reduce burdens

* The number in parentheses represents the number of groups that answered the question for this project.

Based on the team's experience in Damaidi, we decided to simplify the process for the meeting in Yangjia. However, we felt that it was good to have started in a rather "complicated" but holistic way rather than oversimplifying. The ranking exercise did not pose a problem. Although we did not have enough information for our "own" evaluation (according to plan), the meeting benefited local people. The team managed to explain the project and its logic, as well as motivating the villagers. For future meetings, we thought that it might be a good idea to train suitable people to help with facilitation.

Village feedback meeting in Yangjia: The plan for this meeting was as follows.
- Step 1: Presentation of group activities.
- Step 2: Group discussions. The team intended to explain why group discussionsand teamwork are important. We were hoping to find two reliable people (e.g., the village leader and the man who managed the tea nursery), and explain to them the process of group discussions and their logic and ask them to help facilitate. For the discussions, the team planned to divide the villagers into three groups, each discussing four project activities, thinking about the benefits they bring, then selecting their favourite project, and explaining why.
- Step 3: Presentation of results. The team aimed to ask the villagers whether they agreed or disagreed with the results.
- Step 4: Wrap up by discussing other activities considered to be more suitable.

On the day the meeting was scheduled, it rained all day. The village leader warned that people would not come because the paths were very steep and dangerous in the dark when they were slippery. Postponing the meeting to the next day was not possible because it was market day. Only six or seven people made it to the evening meeting and most of them had been among those planning the peach tree project the previous night. They explained that although people knew that the project was good, they were sometimes lazy. Also, most of the men were doing off-farm work at that time, and women alone with children could not leave their houses empty at night. The participants had mainly come to put their names on a list. They made excuses, but did not really see that village meetings were important and thought they could just come and order trees.

The villagers and team had a long discussion about sustainable development, about the process that PARDYP project team wanted to initiate, about the importance of group meetings and sharing and working together. The team explained that we were not there to collect shopping lists. Frustration arose because the soybean activity still had to be planned before the team left, and we still had many questions. Should only the people who attended the meeting be included in the soybean project? How could they plan for the others? Wouldn't that make it too easy for them? The PARDYP team could not just accept orders for plants, because we would be the ones taking the risk. If the project was not well planned and included everyone, the PARDYP team would risk losing a lot of money!

The team asked the villagers present how they could help start the self-development process in the village. The village head said that he would do everything he could to organize a meeting the next morning and make sure a lot of people attended. He would also finish drawing a map of the soybean extension project with farmers. He asked the team to be patient and assured them that people would start understanding the project little by little and would begin participating more and more. He explained that the process was very different from anything they were used to. Usually, government officials would come to the village to talk only to him and he would have to pass the orders on to the others, e.g., "develop 200 mu for walnuts."

The villagers made drawings to illustrate the two approaches. The drawings showed that they thought both the government and PARDYP brought them benefits, but the government forced them to accept and follow its ideas whereas PARDYP did not try to force anyone. Villagers thought that the PARDYP team wanted to do things together so that the villagers could do them alone later. They also understood that the PARDYP team was interested in knowing details about the various activities to make sure that the project would be successful. On the other hand, they depicted government staff as coming to the villages only when the villagers were doing things. Government staff were not concerned about whether the project was successful; in contrast, in the eyes of the villagers, the PARDYP team seemed to care about their success.

Following this enlightening presentation, the team asked the villagers if they thought other farmers felt the same way. The village leader replied that other farmers might think differently at the beginning, but after they learned more about the project they would certainly agree. He pointed out that he had not trusted the team in the beginning, because of many previous problems with outsiders. The team explained that this was exactly why we found group meetings important.

As the team was unsure about attendance at the next morning's meeting, we decided to provide feedback on the activities and ask the current participants to be prepared to share the results with other farmers if the morning meeting was cancelled. The team made the usual presentation with careful details about where the activities took place, the methods, PRA, PTD, the research process, etc. One of the women was astonished at the extent of the activities, and the other farmers all thought the presentation was very interesting. They were particularly impressed by the pig sheds and how many pigs could be raised that way.

The village leader reminded the villagers that the PARDYP team was not the government and that they had to understand that it could not do everything they wanted and that it did not have a great deal of money. However, the team had already done many good things. Everything was also planned carefully. He told the other farmers that if they also planned carefully, then PARDYP might support their activities in the third year of the project. He speculated that PARDYP might be able to help establish a development base for nut trees.

Returning to the soybean project, the village leader had a good idea. The previous year he had planted soybeans on his land. Given that PARDYP would provide a new generation of seeds this year, he wanted to continue planting the "first" variety for comparison and to find out for how many years or generations the seeds could keep producing well. He had also considered the sustainability of the peach tree project. He learned that peach trees produce a good crop for 3 years, but after that production decreases. He had allowed for this by planting different species in his courtyard, so that if the peach trees did not keep producing well, he could graft other species onto them.

Many people came to the second meeting the next morning. The team followed the plan, but divided the participants into two large groups for the discussions, one facilitated by Qian Jie, the other by Yang Lixin. They had prepared two panels with a drawing of all the activities with ample space for writing. A circle in the centre allowed participants to indicate which they thought best.

Qian Jie facilitated a women's group. A high school girl, who had been interviewed the previous day, was asked to be the recorder. The women discussed all of the activities, and Qian Jie answered their questions. They were then asked to choose one preferred activity and discuss it in more detail. Because they were reluctant to do this as a group, each woman was asked to state her preference; all chose activities involving either pigs or chickens. Everyone in Yang Lixin's mixed group went straight to the panels to record their preference and provide reasons, which Yang Lixin wrote in the various boxes. Both groups finished at exactly the same time and the two facilitators presented the results. Finally, Qian Jie briefly repeated who the team members were, why they were carrying out this exercise, how it would contribute to the project, and the reason for this approach.

Planning new activities

Yangjia: The team planned two projects — planting soybeans and peach trees — on the first night during a meeting with all the farmers who had upland fields. Thirty-eight households were going to take part in the soybean extension project and each required 2.5 to 10 kg of seed.

When planning the peach tree project, the team started by reminding the farmers how most of the pear trees that had been planted in the village previously had been stolen. We asked for suggestions on how they could make sure people would not steal the peach trees. The villagers replied that they were going to impose penalties for stealing, and the village head suggested painting the trees. The team asked them to draw a map of all the fields, showing the farmers' names, the size of their land, and the number of trees they wanted to plant. The total area for the trees came to 23.8 mu and about 1 000 trees were needed.

We then discussed management, support needed, and problems that might occur. Farmers asked for technical support concerning cutting and grafting techniques, the use of pesticides and fertilizer, removal of the flowers and collection of the fruit, and early maturation of fruit (to be the first on the market). They also mentioned market studies and advice on what they can intercrop with the trees.

After completing the map, several women went outside to chat and then left. Immediately, the village head told the men they could now start discussing the rules and would be able to think better as it was quieter! They decided to set a fine of 500 – 1 000 RMB for stealing trees, and all participants would have to support the other households in looking for the stolen trees. To benefit other people in the community, they decided to provide branches to other households and even to other people in the valley.

Lijiasi: Zhao Mingshou (of the Baoshan Forestry Bureau) and Yang Lixin described planting and watering techniques. When many new people arrived, Qian Jie suggested that someone who had listened carefully to the explanation could repeat the information. At first no one volunteered, but then one of the officials of the Lijiasi administrative village spoke, describing the technical aspects of the activity. He also mentioned possible conflicts over land boundaries and asked farmers to respect the decisions of the village committee, because they would be for the good of all. He stressed that villagers will have to establish rules about plot boundaries so that farmers do not plant trees too close to each other.

Farmers all wanted to know if it would be possible to plant the peach trees a little closer than usual to take advantage of the characteristics of the species (matures earlier, tastes good and is attractive). Then they discussed management. Again, the most important issue was preventing people from stealing the new species. Although local institutions already existed for dealing with stealing from farmers' lands, a woman said that the rules should be revised and communicated to all households. Women were more eager than men in speaking out about rules.

The new fines that the group established were:
- For stealing a tree or plant: RMB ¥ 300
- For stealing one branch: RMB ¥ 150
- For trespassing by livestock: RMB ¥ 5 per step
- For trespassing by poultry: RMB ¥ 10 per animal
- For trespassing by people: RMB ¥ 50
- For each piece of stolen fruit: RMB ¥ 10

Then, the farmers discussed how to implement the regulations. Eventually, to encourage people to speak up when they witness stealing or trespassing, they decided that the witness would get 30% of the fine, the landowner would get 15%, and the village committee 55%. The later sum would be used to buy fertilizers, tools, etc., for the project. At the end of the meeting, the team decided who would plant how many trees, but because it was late, we did not have time to establish a monitoring and evaluation system.

Second round of meetings to plan the new activities and further monitoring

In 2001, the PARDYP team carried out a second round of meetings. The main results are presented below, followed by some reflections on the whole process.

Damaidi: In Damaidi, the team planned to monitor the tea nursery; check survival rate and discuss how to organize the distribution of plants; monitor the goat ("passing the gift") and pig shed projects; and organize a village meeting to evaluate the water conservation project, plan farmer-to-farmer training in walnut grafting techniques, and explain the technology for establishing high value marketable wild vegetable (*cilabao*) nurseries.

The survival rate of the tea plants was about 80%. Most of the plants were already on order, but often by farmers from other villages. To increase the benefit within the area, the woman implementing this activity decided to give priority to local farmers when selling the plants. An important factor in this project was water supply. Most plants can only be transplanted after 1 year, and water supply must be ensured until then. The team discussed this issue with the authorities in Lijiasi, who agreed to continue providing extra water at preferential rates.

The number of goats in the "passing the gift project" was now 16, and the farmer managing the activity was still very happy. The only issue he raised was that this new species was more susceptible to disease. The revised monitoring and evaluation indicators were: good-looking, smooth fur, fat and strong; high market value; and more people prefer to raise this new variety. The team did not discuss the possibility of "passing the gift" earlier, as Zhao Mingshou thought it was better to adhere to the original contract.

In the pig shed project, the frequency of disease was much lower and the litter size had doubled.

Indicators selected by the local farmers for evaluating the water conservation system were more time available for other work, increased yield, and improvement of the local environment, as the water would stay in the tanks instead of causing erosion. To prepare for the village meeting, the team discussed how to assess these indicators. To measure the difference in available time before and after using the water tanks, they thought of using an H-form or frame, which provides a scale along the middle bar with space for recording reasons along the uprights (Guy and Inglis 1999). Although maize had not yet been harvested, the team could compare the yield of wheat for 2000 and 2001, before and after the water tanks had been built. To evaluate overall perception of the project, they thought of using a drawing of three faces (happy, neutral, sad) (see chapter 4 for an example of the use of this tool). The final step would be to discuss the possibility of building bamboo tanks as a follow-up.

For the farmer-to-farmer training, the team wanted to discuss when the training should take place, identify the local experts or trainers, the kind of technical support required (if any), and the participants (women-men balance). To introduce the technology for establishing cilabao nurseries, we planned to ask villagers if they would be interested in learning about it, present the projects carried out in Lijiasi and Yangjia, and explain how to establish such nurseries.

The meeting took place at the school, in the evening. More than 30 people attended. The team explained their purpose for being there, then went on to the planned agenda.

To evaluate the water conservation project, the team began by discussing the indicators chosen earlier by the local farmers. Most thought that "Improvement of the local environment" should be removed from the list, but no other indicators were added. However, when invited to use the H-form, the farmers seemed reluctant. One finally took the initiative and voiced his opinion on how to measure labour saved. He drew two columns with the number of working days needed to grow maize before building the water tanks on the left side and, on the right, the number of working days needed after building the tanks. He added a third column to show that he had also saved 6 kg of seeds (he had previously needed 18 kg for his field, but this year he had to buy only 12 kg). Then all the farmers who had built water tanks on their land also reported how many working days they needed before and after. For most, the number days decreased by at least half (e.g., from 10 to 4 days, from 30 to 15, 20 to 10). This year, they had only used the water in the tanks on maize as there was not enough for the wheat crop as well. As the maize had not been harvested, we were unable to measure the yield.

During this process, the amount of seed saved was added as a new indicator. Before building the tanks, villagers had to plant the seed directly into the soil and many plants would die or grow at a different paces and heights. Now, with better access to water, they could first plant the seed in small bags, then transplant them to the fields. This resulted in a more uniform crop, increased the survival rate, and decreased the amount of seed purchased.

Regarding the possibility of building bamboo tanks, farmers said they preferred the cement ones, as they are dug into the ground, are stronger, last longer than the bamboo ones (which frequently leak), and cost about the same amount. Bamboo tanks are no cheaper, because they require the knowledge of craftsmen and bamboo is not available to everyone in the village.

Altogether, the farmers were very impressed with the program. Those who had participated wanted to build more tanks and were interested in building a large pond. Those who had not taken part in the program all wanted to build small tanks in their fields. Whether the program motivated them enough to carry on building tanks on their own, without external funding would have to be evaluated in the future.

Regarding farmer-to-farmer training in grafting of fruit trees, almost everyone in the village now knew how to do this. The farmers said they had learned the techniques from each other and, thus, did not see a need for further training. If they encountered a serious technical problem, they would simply ask a local expert.

The farmers agreed that this type of meeting was useful. The discussions increased their enthusiasm and made them think carefully about their various activities. They thought the time and place were appropriate and would like to have more meetings in the future. The project team learned that because PM&E involves the participation of many households, it might be a good idea to establish a group of local people who could be trained in facilitation skills and with whom the team could work to select or design appropriate monitoring and evaluation tools for new projects. The team could then avoid using tools that were too abstract, especially when applied to large groups. With a local group, we could discuss the development of the project and the approach to adopt during visits to the village.

In Lijiasi: In Lijiasi, the team planned to monitor the cilabao nursery and the peach tree project. We also wanted to prepare a detailed management plan for the peach tree project and identify indicators for monitoring and evaluation. We wanted to discuss the project implementation process to date, find out whether any problems had emerged, and ask the farmers to think about the various steps in the project and what kinds of external help and technical knowledge they required at each step.

The village meeting took place in the afternoon, next door to the administrative office. About 20 people attended and issues were discussed according to the agenda. Yang Lixin facilitated the meeting with support from the village administrator. Issues raised by the villagers included:

- There was insufficient water for irrigation during the first phase of the project.
- In some fields, leaves turned yellow because not enough fertilizer was applied.
- A manual was needed to show how to recognize the various fruit tree varieties, with details on their yield, quality, and management requirement.

Farmers in Lijiasi and Yangjia established the same management plan: in December, pruning (training requested), in February and March, flower thinning (training requested), and in June, fertilizing. They agreed on four monitoring and evaluation success indicators during the implementation phase: 100% survival rate, enough fertilizer applied, field managed on time according to the steps identified in the plan, trees grow well. For the final phase, they defined the following success indicators: increase in cash income, at least RMB ¥ 1000 income per mu, a yield of at least 10 kg per tree or an income of RMB ¥ 20 per tree, project extension by selling branches to other households with price based on the lowest yield.

In Yangjia: Here, the team hoped to monitor the walnut and *cilabao* nurseries as well as the peach tree project; refine plans for the peach tree project and establish a monitoring and evaluation system; and discuss the soybean project.

In the walnut nursery, 500 trees would have to be grafted before the end of the year and not enough tools were available. In the cilabao nurseries in both Lijiasi and Yangjia, the survival rates were low. However, at the local extension station, where a trial was being carried out, the survival rate was even lower. Further research and experimentation on the techniques for establishing these nurseries seems to be required.

The wasteland management project was successful. The farmer in charge had already sold half the year's plants for a total of RMB ¥ 300. He and his family harvested a considerable amount of honey for their own consumption and to sell, generating RMB ¥ 500 in income. The income raised from selling rabbits was RMB ¥ 700; the family kept 30 for their own use. They also sold one pig for RMB ¥ 988. On the other hand, the fish pond was a failure, as the water temperature was too low. The chickens had been badly managed, and most had died during the rains or were eaten by dogs or rats. In the following year, the farmer was planning to start planting tangerines and mulberries.

The purpose and agenda for the village meeting were the same as in Lijiasi. The meeting took place at the village leader's house, and about 15 people attended. Zhao Mingshou of the Baoshan Forestry Department took an active role in facilitation. The following issues were raised:

- Some trees had been stolen by outsiders, and the villagers were unable to find the guilty parties. They had decided to use local peach tree varieties to fill the gaps and graft branches from the new variety onto them next year.
- Some trees had developed "black spot disease" because of the high humidity and unstable weather.
- Some leaves had been eaten by pests.

The monitoring and evaluation success indicators selected for the implementation phase included: good community management, a survival rate of 100%, and no stealing of trees. For the final phase, the success indicators selected were: a survival rate of 70% – 90%, a cash income of RMB ¥ 500 per tree, good market value, and development of a good market strategy (e.g., picking the fruits together with leaves to get a higher price).

The team also discussed the soybean extension project, which, unfortunately, had had to be postponed.

Xizhuang: In Xizhuang, the wasteland management and rehabilitation projects were monitored.

Reflections

The introduction of PM&E together with PTD into the project cycle is still at a very early stage, making it difficult to draw well-defined conclusions. Instead, we are looking at what succeeded and what went wrong, and discussing the skills we still need to acquire as well as the management changes we might have to make to strengthen the process. What is certain is that the PARDYP field staff now realize the usefulness of integrating a monitoring and evaluation system into project management to improve quality. The introduction of PM&E to the PTD process has also forced us to reflect on the mistakes we have made in previous projects. For example, when discussing the site rehabilitation project in Xizhuang, one team member mentioned that project staff should spend more time explaining the aims of the project to farmers and discussing issues with them. As a result, management of the site has changed from a research activity undertaken by outsiders on communal land to on-farm experiments on private land. The activities are based on the needs and desires of the farmers, who are now much more willing to take part in planning and management.

We learned that we should try to plan and allow more time for participatory activities before the (PTD) projects are implemented. In each project, a basis for long-term participation should be established. We also learned that PM&E helps spread the risk of failure between the project team and farmers. In too many previous cases, the project bore all the risk and, therefore, farmers did not care enough about managing the activities well. At the beginning, the farmers and project team should establish a protocol to determine indicators of success, identify who will benefit and how if the project is successful, and establish penalties for project failure caused by bad management.

The introduction of PM&E was accompanied by improvement in the management of projects, and in the quality of our reports and the information gathered in the field. Although we see the advantages of PM&E, we are still unsure how to adequately integrate it into long-term research activities; it might be more suited for small-grant community development projects. As we have described in this chapter, several of the PARDYP staff have now experimented with PM&E methods, but more time and effort are needed to make them a natural part of our research efforts.

The institutionalization of PM&E : For PM&E to be efficient, it must be institutionalized at each level of project management and all stakeholders must understand its benefits. The PARDYP team had attempted to introduce itself and the project goals during the January 2000 participatory planning meetings; however, only a few people attended those meetings. Thus, the PM&E concepts were first introduced during the February feedback meetings and discussions. Although these meetings were successful in raising people's interest in our project and motivating them to take part in it, they also highlighted the fact that much more time and effort has to be directed at gaining the trust of local people and building common vision of overall goals. A few meetings are not sufficient.

The February meetings showed that better understanding could be the real motivating force for future participation. We also learned that institutionalizing participatory project management at the village level would take time. It will require empowering local people and changing the process of top-down decision-making to a multistakeholder-based, horizontal one. This, in turn, will require the institutionalization of participatory methods among our local government partners. Many initiatives have already been undertaken in that direction within the Baoshan government, e.g., with staff from the hydrology bureau. PARDYP's first year (1996) was also dedicated to identifying who would be our local partners and to building collaborative relations with them. However, more effort is required at the administrative and village levels. PM&E should build on existing community institutions and integrated into the local governance structure and political process. It is noteworthy that in accordance with the "National Village Organic Law," at the end of the year 2000, local villagers had democratically elected village committees in the whole watershed. The "National Village Organic Law" promotes democratic elections, decision-making, management and monitoring of village activities and expenditures.

But first PM&E must be institutionalized within our own project management. For this to happen, we need to improve communication among PARDYP staff, especially between community development and research staff; we need to learn from each other, share lessons learned from mistakes, and give each other advice. We also need to install a participatory system for monitoring and evaluating our own PM&E process. For example, one of the initial goals for our PM&E was "to enhance the self-development capacity of local participants." However, so far PM&E has been mainly a tool of our own staff. We should discuss how it can be used to empower local people. This would have helped us avoid the conflict that recently emerged over the budget for the water conservation program. If we had shown people how to design their own projects from the beginning, they could have modified the budget themselves or prepared a new, detailed one. Now it is too late, as they have already implemented the activity.

Finally, the work done so far leads us to think that PM&E mechanisms should also be introduced into our other research activities. PARDYP has been studying the soil erosion and hydrology cycle of the Xizhuang watershed for more than 4 years now, and we have never established indicators for deciding when the information collected is "good enough" to use to plan concrete action. PM&E could thus increase the accountability of researchers to the local communities. In Yangjia, at one of our February meetings, a local group mentioned that they did not know what benefits the hydrology studies could bring them. It is time to clear the air (*water*) on this question.

4. "Now we manage our water well": monitoring natural resource use in Guizhou

This and the following chapter describe the experiences of the Guizhou Academy of Agricultural Sciences (GAAS) team. As we did for the PARDYP team in chapter 3, we first follow the GAAS team's attempts to put the detailed PM&E plan for water resource management (prepared during the first training workshop) into practice. In chapter 5, we discuss how the insights and skills gained in this process helped the team take on an additional challenge: a participatory end-of project evaluation to explore the possibility of scaling up the community-based natural resource management approach and methods developed by the team during the last 6 years.

We implemented our draft plan in two villages, Dabuyang and Dongkou. Based on the promising results of this work, we amplified our efforts by including two more villages, Xiaozhai and Chaoshan. By then, local farmers had become major actors in the self-monitored water management system. We report on this exciting experiment and, finally, reflect on the process, achievements, shortcomings, and challenges.

Outcome of the first PM&E training workshop

During the first workshop, which was held in Guiyang, 20 – 23 July 1999, the GAAS team gained a basic understanding of the three key concepts (participation, monitoring, and evaluation), the six basic questions (why, for whom, what, who, how, and when), and the principles for identifying indicators and choosing measurement tools (see chapter 2). Most important, the team recognized that PM&E, as a necessary part of an integrated project cycle, is a continuous process that empowers the local community and builds the capacity of all project stakeholders. The training workshop emphasized the importance of learning by doing, and the fact that the project team should also follow the learning-action-reflection cycle in practicing PM&E. The action plan was based on this principle.

Draft plan for fieldwork

The draft plan was developed mainly by following the six basic questions.

Why: The PM&E fieldwork aimed:

- To promote better understanding and cooperation among the various stakeholders (villagers, local government officials, and the project researchers).
- To identify the problems involved in water management and find solutions and opportunities to improve its effectiveness and efficiency.
- To empower the local community in decision – making, leadership, and management skills.

What: The GAAS project involved a wide range of interventions and research activities regarding the management and use of water, forests, farmland, grassland, and wasteland in six target villages. Because it would be difficult for new practitioners to introduce a PM&E process into such a large project, water management in the villages of Dabuyang and Dongkou was identified as a priority for the first round of fieldwork for the following reasons:

- Water is the most important resource in all six villages because of its scarcity for both drinking and irrigation. The shortage causes great difficulties in the people's daily lives, and all of the villagers set a high priority on water management in their village planning.
- Because of this, the project team put a great deal of effort into research and interventions concerning water management.
- Dabuyang is a Buyi ethnic village, and Dongkou is a Han village. People from different ethnic groups have different perceptions that are influenced by their culture, norms, and customs.
- Dabuyang was a target village since the first phase of the project. Thus 4 1/2 years later, the team considered it necessary to introduce PM&E to assess the effectiveness of the interventions. In phase 2, the project

area expanded to six villages, and Dongkou was among them. Thus, it was chosen for comparison.

Who and for whom: The fieldwork involved the villagers in Dabuyang and Dongkou, the water management staff in both villages, local government officials, and the project researchers. We expected the results to be useful for all these stakeholders.

How: The team paid considerable attention to identifying appropriate indicators, selecting the relevant tools for measuring these indicators, and making arrangements for a number of related activities to share the results.

When: Activities were carefully scheduled as part of the ongoing field research so as not to overload the farmers and officials with additional work. In the remainder of the chapter we present in more detail what happened.

The first round of fieldwork

Introductory workshop: The fieldwork stage began with a workshop at the project site. The objectives were:

- To share information about PM&E with the local villagers and government officials—the concept, the six basic questions, and the menu of methods,
- To obtain some basic information about water management in the two villages,
- To identify appropriate tools and indicators, and
- To establish a shared and adapted action plan for the PM&E fieldwork.

On 10 August 1999, the project team reviewed the information gained at the first PM&E training workshop. Equipped with better understanding of PM&E, the team then discussed and identified a set of criteria for selecting participants for the fieldwork:

- A total of 14 – 16 participants (villagers and government officials)
- Variation among household representatives in terms of economic status and benefit derived from water management
- At least one staff member from the village water management group

● At least one-third female participants

Initially, the workshop was scheduled for early September with fieldwork to follow immediately. However, despite all the planning, both workshop and fieldwork had to be postponed until November for various reasons, some unexpected, others involving harvest time. With the help of the village leaders, we finally selected 14 participants: two government officials (one man, one woman), five villagers from Dabuyang (two women, three men), five from Dongkou (three women, two men), and one (male) member of the management staff from each village. Zhou Pidong, Sun Qiu, Li Zhinan, Yuan Juanwen, Chen Deshou, and Ren Xiaodong made up the GAAS team.

On the day of the workshop (23 November), professor Chen Deshou, the project leader, began by explaining the purpose and importance of the workshop to all participants. Then, using visual aids such as a projector and flipchart, Zhou Pidong (the workshop facilitator) gave a detailed explanation of basic concepts, the six basic questions, and the methods (tools and indicators).

The participants were divided into two groups (one for each village), and the facilitators initiated the discussion by asking two questions: "What has been done on water management in your village since the implementation of the project?" and "What do you think about water management in your village and why?" The villagers and government officials were asked to write or draw their answers on cards. The facilitators helped group the answers and transfer them to a flipchart, where they served as a focus for the in-depth discussions that followed.

The facilitators assisted in the identification of indicators and measurement tools by raising questions and summarizing discussions. For example, some participants said they thought that the water management system in their village was successful. When asked why, they replied that conflicts had decreased. Thus, the number of conflicts could be a criterion for measuring the success or failure of water management; a decrease in conflicts would reflect good management practices.

The main output of the workshop was an improved PM&E plan that

Table 10. Multi-stakeholder framework for PM&E of water management systems (GAAS project team)

	Content	Indicators	Measurement tools	Information sources	FOR WHOM/WHO
Outputs	Utilization of water	Irrigation area Labour needed to collect drinking water	Resource mapping Household interviews	Village leaders and the participating villagers Villagers (women)	• Local communities/villagers • Water management groups • Local government • The research team • Other communities • Other researchers
	Effectiveness of management group and management regulations	Effectiveness of facility operations Distribution of drinking water (Dongkou) Services of the management staff Enforcement of the regulations Improved service Fairness of water distribution	Matrix scoring Group interviews Key informant interviews Semi-structured interviews Self-monitoring book	Participating villagers Village leaders Management staff Researchers	
Outcomes and impacts	Management capacity and villagers' awareness and attitude toward resource use	Frequency of stealing water pipes (Dongkou) Water pumping arrangement for irrigation (Dabuyang) Timeliness of water distribution Ease of water fee collection Number of conflicts over water distribution Labour and fund mobilization in building and maintenance of facilities	Key informant interviews Secondary data	Village cadres Management staff Participating villagers Local households Researchers Local government Village committee	
Reach	Villagers inside and outside the project, local government, project researchers, outside researchers, and visitors	Number of villages influenced Number of visits Number of reports Number of visitors Sharing of experience with other researchers Number of villages that have adopted the project's water management measures	Key informant interviews Secondary data analysis	Village leaders Local government officials Outside researchers Project team members Local households Researchers Local government Village committee	

included a clear idea of the content, indicators, tools, and resource people (Table 10). Even more important, most of the villagers and government officials acquired a good grasp of the purpose and significance of PM&E. By comparing it with conventional monitoring and evaluation, they saw that PM&E is *theirs* and for *themselves*. However, how to practice PM&E and their roles in its implementation still remained unclear to them.

During the discussions, the project team obtained a considerable amount of information about the management of water resources in the two villages. In the evening, the team planned for 2 days of fieldwork based on the framework developed at the workshop (Table 10). It included the establishment of two PM&E teams (one for each village), determining the roles of team members in the field, and scheduling the work according to the indicators and tools (see Table 11).

Table 11. Action plan for the fieldwork of the GAAS project team

Dabuyang team: Zhou Pidong facilitator, Yuan Juanwen assistant facilitator, Chen Deshou observer and collector of secondary data
Dongkou team: Li Zhinan facilitator, Sun Qiu assistant facilitator, Pan Jiawen observer and collector of secondary data

November 24
    ● Morning: Resource mapping, secondary data collection
    ● Afternoon: Group interviews and matrix scoring
    ● Evening: Compare notes and share experiences
November 25
    ● Morning: Household and key informant interviews
    ● Afternoon: Interview Kaizhuo township government officials
    ● Evening: Compare notes and analyze data

Description and results of fieldwork in Dabuyang: On 24 November, the Dabuyang team arrived at the home of the village leader, who was expecting them. She quickly assembled a group of five villagers, two of whom were women. After learning the purpose of the meeting, these seven villagers (including the husband of the village leader) drew a chart to give the team a clear picture of water resource use in the village. The team conducted a group interview focusing on the problems and issues raised during the mapping exercise. In the following discussions, all the villagers agreed that the construction of tap water and irrigation facilities brought them great benefits, including irrigation of about 10 ha of paddy fields, convenient and hygienic drinking water, and a reduction in women's labour as they no longer had to collect drinking water from wells. Indoor plumbing (in 95% of the households) had brought the local villagers a change in life-style; some households had built their own toilets and installed bath facilities. As one villager said, "Now we can live like city residents."

When the team asked about problems, the responses of male and female villagers were quite different. The three women said it was obvious to all villagers that the water facilities in Dabuyang were in good condition and had been operated very well since their establishment about 4 years earlier. The only current problem was that a small number of households did not pay a water fee. One of the reasons, they explained, was a temporary economic difficulty that the households were facing. In contrast, the four men thought that not paying the water fee was a serious problem, which would result in other households refusing to pay unless the village leaders enforced the regulations. Obviously, they were dissatisfied with the current performance of the management staff. However, they all conceded that even in the current problematic situation, the supply of drinking water and the maintenance of the facilities such as pipes and faucets were satisfactory.

The three women suggested that new irrigation facilities should be built for other rain fed paddy fields. To make their point, they showed us the location of these fields on the resource map and where the new irrigation facilities should be built. The four men, on the other hand, thought that this plan was too expensive and that the water supply might be insufficient.

With the help of these seven people, the team selected 12 other villagers (four of whom were women) for a focus-group discussion. At this discussion, which began at about 2:30 p. m. at the home of another villager, the guiding questions were: "What are the problems in the water resource management in Dabuyang?" and "What are the reasons for these problems?" One of the team members recorded the main points on cards and pinned them to a board, which was then used to rank the problems in terms of their importance and urgency (Table 12). Finally, using a matrix scoring method, the 12 villagers were asked to evaluate the effectiveness of the operation of the facilities, the services provided by the management staff, and enforcement of the regulations. The focus-group discussion lasted about 2 hours. During it, the men were quite vocal, but the women remained relatively silent.

Table 12. Ranking of problems in the water management system in Dabuyang and perceived reasons for them

Problems in order of importance and urgency	Main reasons for them
Difficulty in collecting the water fee	The fee collector lacked patience and was irresponsible. Temporary economic difficulty in paying the water fee for some of households.
Lack of management experience and skills among the management staff	Lack of necessary training.
Ever-decreasing enthusiasm of the management staff	Low income from the management and services provided.

The following morning, the team carried out individual interviews with seven villagers focusing on the identified problems. These villagers, who included the informal village leader, the water fee collector, and the clan leader, shared a common understanding of the current problems. Most appreciated the diligent work of the water management staff (one man, one woman); they praised their conscientious attitude and their responsive and good service. They thought that the male staff member was indispensable because he was an acknowledged technical expert in the maintenance of facilities and equipment. On the other hand, they noted, he lacked management experience and skills. For example, he followed a first-come, first-served principle regarding distribution of water for irrigation; thus, when a group of people came to him at the same time, a conflict arose.

The individual interviews revealed important information about the reasons for the problems and why some interviewees were reluctant to speak about water management issues in public. For example, the informal leader thought that current problems could be ascribed to three issues. First, the village leader was also the principal manager, so there was no independent institution to supervise and support the work. Second, regulations had not been properly enforced; in particular, those who failed to pay water fees on time had not been penalized. Third, the management group did not post its financial statements regularly; thus, some villagers suspected the staff of embezzlement, which was a major reason why they were reluctant to pay their water fees. Most of these villagers also reported that the official did not collect the water fee regularly (once a month) as stipulated in the regulations.

According to the informal leader, the water fee collector justified his behaviour by explaining that he could not always collect the fees on schedule as he had to work at other jobs to earn enough money, especially in the slack seasons. In other words, the remuneration was too small in terms of the time and energy required. Three interviewees also mentioned that the water fee collector was not a native of Dabuyang village, but had moved there 6 years previously when he had married a village woman. They explained that the "newcomer" was regarded as belonging to a lower social class and would have difficulty gaining the respect of the local people. Although this might have been an important factor affecting the water fee collection, in further interviews, only a few people seemed to have the same perception. Most did not want to express an opinion on this matter, although no one denied that a problem existed.

According to the agenda, the afternoon was to be devoted to finding solutions for the existing problems and conflicts. To make the discussion more effective, two groups were formed: one with six women and the other with seven men. Their suggestions included choosing new management staff, establishing a subgroup that would share responsibility for water management, revising the regulations to increase remuneration for the management staff, and setting up a special group to support and supervise the work of the management staff.

Description and results of fieldwork in Dongkou: On 24 November, the Dongkou team arrived at the village leader's home where he, the current water manager, and the previous water manager were waiting. Because the three men had all attended the PM&E workshop, they knew the purpose of the fieldwork and were also ready with such relevant information as the records for water-fee collection, penalties, and uses of the collected fees. Together with these villagers, the team examined the information and obtained detailed answers to several questions.

The analysis and discussion revealed the following:

- Construction of the plumbing system had greatly alleviated the problem of collecting drinking water, although the amount of potable water was still insufficient during the dry seasons (from October to April). Most of the women in Dongkou were now freed from the burden of having to collect dinking water every day; this saved them about 1 hour a day.
- Construction of mountain ponds had solved the problem of water shortage for the irrigation of rice seedling paddies.
- Management regulations were strictly enforced from the very beginning. For example, a villager was fined RMB ¥ 10 for using potable water to irrigate rice paddy.
- Village leaders effectively supervised and assisted in the work of the water management staff, especially in resolving conflicts.
- Drinking water came from three sources, all far from the village; thus, protection of water sources and pipes was very difficult for the management staff. The former manager had been dismissed after water pipes were stolen twice, and the new staff person said that he could not handle this problem alone. Both agreed that the support of the village leaders and the villagers was necessary and important in terms of backing up enforcement of regulations and resolving conflicts.
- The new manager mentioned that water distribution among the households in various parts of the village would be a big challenge in the dry seasons.

Together with these three village men, the team identified house location as the criterion for selecting villagers for focus-group discussions in the afternoon. Seven villagers (including three women) were selected: two represented households in the upper part of the village; three, the middle part; and two, the lower part.

Focus-group discussions were conducted in the vice-leader's home beginning at 2:00 p. m. The three women were very positive and excited about the water system; although drinking water was still insufficient in the dry season, women no longer had to walk more than 3 km to get water. In terms of current problems, they focused on the shortage of drinking water and the distribution of water during the dry season. In contrast, the men were more concerned about water for irrigation, which they considered the main factor limiting agricultural production, especially of rice. They suggested building a larger mountain pond to collect rain to supplement groundwater for irrigation of rice paddies. They said that this would require a great deal of money and realized that it would be impossible for the villagers to raise this money by themselves. They planned to apply to the government, but also hoped for a financial contribution from the CBNRM project.

Some villagers also thought that it was difficult for one person to manage the whole drinking water and irrigation system. In addition, villagers whose houses were located in the upper part of the village complained that they often could not get water when the households in the lower part of the village were using tap water. They thought that low water pressure was not the only cause. Table 13 shows the problems and reasons for them as ranked by the villagers present.

In the morning of the following day, two focus-group discussions with seven women and eight men were conducted. The team intended to concentrate on the timing of drinking water supply, the collection of water fees, and managing conflicts; however, the women's group wanted to focus on how to improve the timing problem and finding other water sources to provide adequate drinking water. (Some villagers suggested that water supplies to the three locations should be independent of each other.) As in Dabuyang, the men were more concerned about irrigation water.

Table 13. Ranking of problems in the water management system in Dongkou and perceived reasons for them

Problems in order of importance	Main reasons for them
Extreme shortage of water for irrigation	No major groundwater sources Too far from surface water sources
Insufficient drinking water during dry seasons	Existing water sources insufficient Leakage of water
Lack of protection for pipes and water sources	Three water sources all far from the village
Potential problems: inequitable distribution of drinking water among households in different parts of the village during the dry seasons; maintenance of water facilities	Low water pressure Poor design of the water pipe system Water supply too concentrated (time-wise) Broken pipes Lack of skill for water facilities maintenance

Following these discussions, the team walked through the village along with several villagers to examine the tap water system. Some water leakage was evident due to poor installation. The team also carried out an on-the-spot investigation of the area where the villagers planned to build a larger mountain pond.

In the afternoon, individual interviews were conducted with three other villagers according to the plan, but the results and information were very similar to that obtained in the group interviews.

Visit to the Kaizhuo township office: After the fieldwork in Dabuyang and Dongkou, four members of the project team paid a visit to the Kaizhuo township office, where they had a 1-hour discussion with two township leaders, the head of the extension station for agricultural techniques, and one staff person from the hydraulic station. Discussion focused on the significance and impact of the development and management of water facilities in the two villages.

The township leaders thought that the approach to the development and management of the water facilities adopted in Dabuyang and Dongkou villages was significant. First, it was villager-centred and emphasized the need for the villagers to solve their own problems, which could increase the participation of local people and lighten the financial burden on the government. Second, this approach paid more attention to the management aspect of the use of water, which was often neglected in government projects. The leaders also mentioned that at least five villages had voluntarily adopted this approach, and that the township government was planning to extend it to other projects with the help of the project team.

The other two officials added that Changshun county lacked water resources and facilities. Every year the county government spent a large amount of money building or improving water facilities (mainly for irrigation), but because of ineffective management most of these were in poor condition. The success of Dabuyang and Dongkou in the management and use of water resources had greatly impressed and inspired the leaders and technician from the county's hydraulic bureau.

Feedback and adjustments

On 26 November, all the people who had attended the introductory workshop were invited to a discussion meeting with the project team. The aim was to share information from the fieldwork and discuss the problems and issues surrounding the management and use of water in the two villages. The team members made a detailed presentation of the results of the fieldwork, then the group looked at the information together. After this introduction, the Dabuyang and Dongkou teams conducted separate discussions about the reasons for the problems, then worked out solutions or adjustments.

On 27 November, the two PM&E teams returned to Dabuyang and Dongkou to organize open meetings during which they shared the information from the PM&E fieldwork with the villagers. The village leaders commented on the findings and, based on a discussion of the results, advised the villagers to consider adjustments in the water management system. The following suggestions were made.

Dabuyang village: Regarding collection of water fees, two suggestions were made: replace the fee collector; or set up four new submanagement groups. If the second suggestion was adopted, households sharing the same side of the system would form a subgroup. Every household member would belong to a subgroup and would be responsible for collecting fees for 1 month and for taking care of the water pipes. The management staff would mainly be responsible for supervision of the subgroups and overall maintenance of the facilities. However, most of the villagers preferred the first suggestion, as they were afraid they would not have time to take care of water pipes and collect fees.

Regarding management of the irrigation system, the villagers decided that the principle of charging first, setting priorities, and then supplying water should be adopted to avoid conflicts. One manager would be responsible for collecting the fees and establishing the order, and another for pumping the water. The villagers said they would try this plan, and if it did not work well, they could look for another method.

Dongkou village: Two decisions were made and supported by all the villagers:

- New sources would be found to alleviate the shortage of drinking water. One possibility was in the neighbouring village, but using it would require negotiations. At the same time, the villagers thought it best to build a large mountain pond to increase the supply of irrigation water as much as possible. It was estimated that such a pond could provide water for at least a third of the paddy fields of the village.
- The village households would be divided into two groups according to location (upper and lower areas), and drinking water would be supplied at different times to the two groups.

The project team also had a suggestion. Based on their reading of the interest shown by villagers, they suggested setting up a self-monitoring and evaluation mechanism at the village level using a simple booklet. They proposed that the system be tested in Dabuyang and Dongkou. The team hoped that through daily observation and monitoring, the villagers would be able to collect more timely data to use for making adjustments in the water management, and that this would be an effective local mechanism for problem-solving and decision-making. Villagers and leaders agreed to test the tool.

What we learned at the second PM&E training workshop

In April 2000, the KIB and GAAS teams met in Kunming to share experiences and provide critical feedback about their attempts to carry out PM&E in the field (see chapter 2). The insights, ideas, and comments generated during that workshop helped us draft a plan for the next steps in the fieldwork. The GAAS team realized that further fieldwork was needed to learn more about how to make a useful and meaningful monitoring system work.

The team was also encouraged to expand on its efforts to introduce a self-monitoring instrument in Dabuyang and Dongkou villages. They improved the design and planned to test it in two additional villages. Subsequent fieldwork would continue to focus on water management with emphasis on the efficiency and effectiveness of the system for both drinking water and irrigation in the four villages in terms of service provided by management staff, adequacy of water supply, effectiveness of facility operation, management system and regulations; and the usefulness of the new self-monitoring tool.

In choosing two more villages in which to conduct the new round of PM&E, the following factors were taken into consideration: ethnic group, topography, location (distance to the township), the project phase during which the village became part of the project, the nature and volume of its water supply and the water fee. Table 14 shows a comparison of Dabuyang, Dongkou, and the two new villages (Xiaozhai and Chaoshan) in terms of these factors.

Personnel who would be involved in these activities were: men and women from all four villages, including both households selected for self-monitoring and others; management staff in the four villages (two from Dabuyang, and one each from Dongkou, Xiaozhai, and Chaoshan); two township officials and village leaders (two from Dabuyang, one from Dongkou, two from Xiaozhai, and one from Chaoshan); and project team members Sun Qiu, Zhou Pidong, Yuan Juanwen, Li Zhinan, and Chen Deshou.

Table 14. Characteristics of the four villages involved in the second round of PM&E fieldwork

Factor	Dabuyang	Dongkou	Xiaozhai	Chaoshan
Ethnic group	Buyi	Han	Han	Buyi and Miao
Topography	Valley area	Hilly area	Hilly area	Valley area
No. of households	57	52	24	58
Distance to township	1 km	6 km	5 km	2.5 km
Timing of project involvement	Since phase I	Since phase II	Since phase I	Since phase II
Adequacy of water supply	Sufficient water supply all year round	Insufficient water supply in dry season	Insufficient water supply in dry season	Sufficient water supply all year round
Nature of water supply	Pumped	Gravity-fed	Gravity-fed	Pumped
Water fee rate	RMB ¥ 1.0 /m^3	RMB ¥ 0.7 /m^3	RMB ¥ 0.7 /m^3	RMB ¥ 0.8 /m^3

The second round of fieldwork

Together with village leaders, the project team selected 10 households each in Dabuyang, Dongkou, and Chaoshan and six households in Xiaozhai for self-monitoring (36 households in total, representing 17 – 25% of all household). Selection was based on house location (higher and lower part of the village), economic status as defined locally (high, medium, and low; see Table 15), and size of irrigated field (large, medium, and small). All selected households showed a willingness to take part. The indicators of economic status were defined by the villagers themselves during the participatory rural appraisal carried out by the team in 1998.

Table 15. Locally defined indicators of economic status of households at the GAAS project site (1998)

Economic status	Key indicators
High	Big new house 2 or more cattle or buffaloes Enough labourers in family
Medium	Medium-sized house 1 cattle or buffalo
Low	No cattle or buffalo Small house More children and less labour

The simple, visually oriented self-monitoring booklets were distributed to the selected households, who were asked to provide monthly comments and opinions about the water management system in their village. They were encouraged to use their own indicators for judging the adequacy of the system. Village meetings would be held at 3 – month intervals to review the comments in the booklets, assess the situation, and identify problems in management and the use of the collective fund derived from water fees. It was also agreed that in case of an emergency, villagers would call a meeting immediately.

Toward the end of 2000, the research team conducted focus-group discussions (with men and women separately, and with management staff, households living in similar locations, and village leaders) and key informant interviews (with management staff and households with self – monitoring booklets) to get feedback about the use of the booklets. Several meetings were also held to discuss findings with the villagers.

Dabuyang village: The records from Dabuyang showed that the main problems villagers were facing were a difficulty in collecting water fees and ineffective management of the irrigation system (Table 16).

Table 16. Summary of comments recorded in self-monitoring booklets by 10 households in Dabuyang, 2000

	☺	😐	☹	Problem	Measures taken to solve problem
January	·	· · · ·	· · · · ·	Difficulty in water fee collection	
February	·	· · · ·	· · · · ·	Difficulty in water fee collection	
March		· · · · ·	· · · · ·	Difficulty in water fee collection	Change management staff（staff）
April		· · ·	· · · · · · ·	Difficulty in water fee collection, busy season, staff is not willing to manage irrigation water	Villagers taught each other to operate pumping station
May		· · · ·	· · · · · ·	Busy season, staff is not willing to manage irrigation water	Villagers operate pumping station by themselves
June		· · · ·	· · · · · ·	Busy season, staff is not willing to manage irrigation water	Villagers operate pumping station by themselves
July	· · · ·	· · · ·	· ·	Staff has no incentive to collect water fee due to the low return	Staff and villagers suggest employing contract manager for water and electricity
August	· · · · ·	· · ·	· ·	Staff has no incentive to manage water and collect water fee due to the low return	Staff and villagers suggest employing contract manager for water and electricity
September	· · · ·	· · · · ·	·	Staff has no incentive to collect water fee due to the low return	Staff and villagers suggest employing contract manager for water and electricity
October	· · · · ·	· · · · ·		Staff has no incentive to collect water fee due to the low return	Staff villagers suggest employing contract manager for water and electricity
November	· · · · ·	· · · · ·		Staff has no incentive to collect water fee due to the low return	Staff and villagers suggest employing contract manager for water and electricity
December	· · · · ·	· · · · ·		Staff has no incentive to collect water fee due to the low return	Staff and villagers suggest employing contract manager for water and electricity

The water management staff in Dabuyang consisted of two people: one in charge of pumpingwater and facility maintenance; the other of fee collection. The latter position had been held by three people, a woman (who was replaced when she became village leader in 1999), followed by two men.

Toward the end of 2000, the project team met with the two village leaders, one of whom was also a member of the water management staff. Asked about constraints they were facing in terms of water management, the two leaders agreed that the most difficult task was collecting fees, especially for irrigation water (including an electricity charge). One of the leaders explained that this problem arose with the selection of the previous fee collector in 1999 (see section on the first round of fieldwork in Dabuyang). The collector had little incentive to collect the fees because his remuneration for the job was very low. The leaders also pointed out that most of the villagers were relatives; every time they organized a meeting to discuss this issue, most people kept silent because they did not want to criticize their brothers, uncles, sons, etc., who owed water fees. This was compounded by the fact that the village leader with water management duties was a kind, gentle man who was unwilling to "get tough" with the villagers who did not pay their fees. This situation was making villagers who did pay on time very unhappy. The two leaders agreed that without the villagers' support and understanding, they could not work out a solution to these problems.

Before the team left, the leader with water management duties told us he did not want to fill both positions anymore. He explained that although he had tried his best to work for the common good of the village, he was disappointed with the result and suggested that someone else in village take on the water management job.

Later, the team interviewed three households that still owed water fees. The woman from the first household said that she did not like owing the money, but she simply had no money. She said she would pay it after the rapeseed harvest. In the second household, a man told us, "If the previous collector had come to collect the water fee monthly, I might have had money to pay. But he came every 3 months or more, so how possibly could I have such a large sum of

· 114 ·

money to pay?" When asked what he planned to do now, he replied that he would look for a job in the city during the rainy season and hope that he made enough money to pay the fee. At the third household, a woman shouted at us, "I will pay if the others pay."

The previous water fee collector was not in the village at the time of the team's visit, but they interviewed the new collector. He reported, "I collected water fees every month. Normally there was no problem to collect potable water fees which are only RMB ¥ 5 – 10 a month per household. Some households had no money at hand, I would pay for them first and they would pay me back when they had money. I could do this because they felt that they owed me personally instead of owing the village. However, for the irrigation water fee, I could not afford to pay for them first. That was too expensive. Usually I pumped water for them after they paid. But in a dry year, like this year, the villagers needed water so badly for raising and transplanting rice-seedlings. I could hardly refuse to pump water for them when they came to me without paying money. Most of them paid the fee after rice harvesting, but some did not until now. Yes, I broke the rule, but I had no choice. I could not bear seeing my co-villagers hungry because I did not pump water for them."

When asked how the water management system could be improved, he suggested a "contract management system," in which the management function would be contracted out to one person or a group of people. According to the fee collector this might solve the fee problem because "people normally think it is all right to owe money to the state, the county, the township and the village, but not to a private person or a private group."

A group discussion was arranged for the evening, and nine villagers (four women and five men) attended. Most of these villagers admitted that a contract management system might be a good alternative. However, when they were asked who would be willing to take on the task without increasing the water fee rate, they were silent. Another unanswered question was whether poor households would still benefit from the water system under a contract management system.

Xiaozhai village : The self-monitoring booklets from Xiaozhai showed that most of the selected households were very satisfied with water management in their village despite the fact that for half the year (July to December) the main pipes were leaking in four places (Table 17). Puzzled by this, the project team organized two group meetings, one with village women and one with men. During the meetings, no one wanted to discuss the leaking pipes; the villagers only admitted that "no one took care of the leaking pipes and we do not know why this is." The team felt that this must be a sensitive issue; to try to learn more, they approached the villagers, water management staff, and the village leaders individually.

Table 17. Summary of comments recorded in self-monitoring booklets by 6 households in Xiaozhai (2000)

	☺	😐	☹	Problem	Measures taken to solve problem
January	·····	·			
February	·····	·			
March	·····	·			
April	······				
May	······				
June	······				
July	····	··		Pipes leaked	
August	···	···		Nobody takes care of the leaking pipes, difficulty in water fee collection	Need support from township government
September	·····	·			
October	···	···			
November	·	····	·	Nobody takes care of the leaking pipes	Need support from village leader
December	··	····		Tap broken	

The water manager said that he had noticed the leaking pipes and had tried to fix them; however, some leaks were too deep for him to fix on his own. Although he had then reported this matter to the village leader several times, asking him to mobilize the villagers to repair the pipes, the leader did not take the matter seriously. The manager told the team that many water fees had not been paid, and he had not received any remuneration for almost half a year. He went on to point out another problem underlying the unwillingness of villagers to pay their fees: the village leader's brother, who ran the mill, refused to submit payment for this contract and, in retaliation several villagers had refused to pay their water fees.

Intrigued by this situation, the team then interviewed the village leader. He complained that the villagers did not understand and support him. He had called village meetings several times, but no one attended. He had asked the villagers to repair the leaking pipes, but no one had listened. He did not seem to know why, although he later suggested that the villagers might be blaming him for his brother's behaviour. As a step toward solving this problem, he agreed to urge his brother to respect the milling contract.

The team also interviewed 10 households chosen at random. Most were unhappy with the village leader, citing his unfairness and selfishness. They explained that the village leader had three brothers, one of whom was the local communist party secretary, so they were the most powerful family in the village. The interviewees thought that there was little transparency in the management of village affairs. They wanted very much to replace the village leader and hoped for support in this from the township government. Later, when the team reported this situation to the township leaders, they promised to look into it.

Dongkou village: Overall, people in Dongkou were satisfied with their water management system (see Table 18). They said that the management staff was very responsible. The current manager checked the water pipes every day and none had been stolen. The manager ensured that the water supply was adequate and distributed equitably to households in different locations. He had gained the villagers' respect for his good service and commitment. Village leaders were committed to enforcing the management regulations and regularly reported on the use and management of the fees. The villagers trusted them and supported their work. The only problem was that there was not enough water in the dry season. The villagers had built two holding ponds in the mountains the previous year, and were now looking for new water sources.

Table 18. Summary of comments recorded in self-monitoring booklets by 10 households in Dongkou (2000)

	🙂	😐	🙁	Problem	Measures taken to solve problem
January		• • •	• • • • • • •	Insufficient water supply	Looking for new water source
February		• •	• • • • • • • •	Insufficient water supply	Same
March	•	• • •	• • • • • •	Insufficient water supply	Same
April	• • • • • • • •	• •		Good service of management staff	
May	• • • • • • • • • •			Good service of staff	
June	• • • • • • • • •	•		Good service of staff	
July	• • • • • • • • •	•		Good service of staff	
August	• • • • • • • • •	•		Good service of staff, strict regulation enforcement	
September	• • • • •	• • • • •		Dry season starts, beginning of water supply problem	
October	•	• • • • • • •	• •	Insufficient water supply	
November		• •	• • • • • • • •	Insufficient water supply	
December		• •	• • • • • • • •	Insufficient water supply	

Chaoshan village: Chaoshan had the largest management group: two village leaders and five villagers, elected by the village assembly and representing the two ethnic groups, Miao and Buyi, and the various clans. The group handled both water and electricity management contracts and had outlined clear responsibilities for each member. From group discussions and key informant interviews, the project team learned that villagers rated their service as excellent (Table 19) and they appreciated the low cost. The village also provided free potable water to the poorest family.

However, some villagers mentioned that the management group did not report regularly about use of the water fees. Both men and women villagers suggested that the management group should be more accountable. Representing the management group, the village leader remarked during a feedback meeting that they would let the villagers know where every penny of the water fee went.

Table 19. Summary of comments recorded in self-monitoring booklets by 10 households in Chaoshan (2000)

	😊	😐	🙁	Problem	Measures taken to solve problem
January	· · · · · · · · · ·			Good service, reasonable price	
February	· · · · · · · · · ·			Same	
March	· · · · · · · · · ·			Same	
April	· · · · · · · · · ·			Same	
May	· · · · · · · · · ·			Same	
June	· · · · · · · · · ·			Same	
July	· · · · · · · · · ·			Same	
August	· · · · · · · · · ·			Same	
September	· · · · · · · · · ·			Same	
October	· · · · · · · · · ·			Same	
November	· · · · · · · · · ·			Same	
December	· · · · · · · · · ·			Same	

Issues emerging from the fieldwork

An important issue that emerged from the two rounds of fieldwork was the need to identify appropriate indicators in PM&E. According to theory, the indicators must be "SMART": specific, measurable, attainable, relevant, and timely. The team attempted to put theory into practice by identifying meaningful indicators, defined by the local water users. It organized a workshop in the villages to work out the PM&E operational framework, which included indicators agreed on by the farmer participants. Later, based on answers to the question "Why are you satisfied (not satisfied)?" in the self-monitoring booklet, the team produced a set of indictors to measure the efficiency and effectiveness of water management (Table 20). We are planning to include these indicators and subindicators in a revised version of the booklets.

Table 20. Villagers' indicators of effective and efficient water management
(GAAS project)

Objective	Indicator	Subindicator
Efficiency and effectiveness of water management	Quality of the service provided by management staff	Regular water supply Timely repairs of broken pipes and taps
	Efficiency of the operation of the water facility	Who operate the facility: management staff pumps irrigation water or the villagers do it by themselves Fairness of water distribution
	Effectiveness of the enforcement of regulations	Ease of fee collection Transparency in water management/regular reporting about water fee use

A second issue was the usefulness of the self-monitoring booklet. This had been the first step in an attempt to establish a self-monitoring system for natural resource management in the community. However, although the self-monitoring booklet did reflect some useful information, it did not capture all the relevant facts. Moreover, the booklet mainly served as a recording device; it did not function as a tool for solving problems, as we had expected. Furthermore, the booklet was not gender sensitive; it failed to capture the *possibly* different views and interests of the men and women in a household. We realized this when we asked, "Who normally fills in the booklet?" Men recorded the marks and observations in two-thirds of all cases. This shortcoming made us more aware that we need to carefully look into the *underlying* factors and dynamics that shape gender roles, interests and positions.

Several factors contributed to problems in the use of the booklets. First, except in Dongkou, no regular village meetings were held where villagers could review the results of the monitoring efforts and decide what action to take to solve problems. In Chaoshan, villagers claimed that they had no problems, so they did not hold meetings. In Dabuyang, the village leader wanted to resign but no one else wanted to be leader. In Xiaozhai, villagers paid no attention to the village leader because of his poor reputation. Second, several of the households that maintained booklets expressed worry about the possibility of getting into trouble if they recorded all the facts; no one wanted their name on the booklet. Third, a few households did not take the booklet seriously; and did not fill in the form until we asked to see the booklets.

Lessons learned

Regular village meetings to evaluate the efficiency and effectiveness of water management are crucial for making timely and appropriate adjustments. The self-monitoring booklet has the potential not only to serve as a documentation tool, but as an instrument for identifying problems and suggesting solutions. As we discussed, the booklet could be improved in terms of recording precision through more detailed indicators and a comparison of annotations made by women and men.

Our experience seems to suggest that village leaders should not also be members of the water management staff for two reasons. When villagers misunderstand or have a conflict with management staff, no third party representing village leadership is available to help solve the problem. Also, trying to be village leader, water management staff member, and parent simultaneously involves too much work and responsibility.

Increasing accountability of management is an important factor influencing villagers' participation and the effectiveness of the management system. During the study, we noticed that villages in which the leadership did not regularly report on use of village funds had problems with water fee collection. As one villager in Xiaozhai said, "Nobody likes the idea to give money to the water management staff without knowing where the money goes to and for what."

Conclusions

Through the training workshops and fieldwork, we have come to recognize the important roles that PM&E can play. At the GAAS project site, PM&E helped the water users, project researchers, and local government officials work together to identify problems as well as opportunities and strategies for improving effectiveness and efficiency of the water management system. At the same time, PM&E helped build capacity, accountability, and confidence about adequate water management. Dongkou villagers stated this eloquently: "Everybody in the village cares about water management and makes efforts to maintain the facilities and implement the management regulations. Now we can also manage our own resources well."

There is no fixed model for participatory monitoring: different villages have different interests, and different geographic, economic, and political contexts. As work in the four villages demonstrated, villagers have a unique cultural background and social system (networks, values, rules) and are dealing with a variety of changing natural and political conditions. Introducing and using PM&E requires an open mind, flexibility and a step-by-step approach.

We learned that water management consists not only of managing the water (a technical matter), but is also very much related to sociocultural and economic issues and power/ knowledge configurations and dynamics. In Dabuyang, the former water fee collector had difficulty collecting fees "simply" because he was not Buyi and not respected by the villagers. Chaoshan had a large, but very effective, management group selected by the villagers from both Buyi and Miao groups and it was endorsed by important clans in the village. Management staff represented a variety of interests, and this seemed to be instrumental in their relatively smooth performance.

Despite the progress we believe we have made, we still face difficulties in practicing PM&E in the field, especially in ensuring the continuity of the process. We must continue the learning process. We also feel that there is a need for further research into appropriate participatory tools, the development and testing of suitable indicators, and the development of training materials. We have learned that PM&E is not just an add-on activity; it should be an integral part of the entire project. Thus, institutionalization of PM&E must become a priority. In particular, institutionalization of self-monitoring requires much more effort from researchers and farmers, as well as local government officials.

5. "Realizing our dreams": participatory project evaluation in Guizhou

In chapter 4, we described the GAAS team's efforts to establish a participatory monitoring system for water management. During discussions with program staff at the Ford Foundation and IDRC, the team started to think about how to build on these achievements and the lessons learned and to expand the CBNRM approach and methods. As noted by John Graham, an IDRC program officer who was involved in these discussions, "Many projects have been quite successful at working in communities or with farmers, but many of these grassroots successes and approaches are not being integrated into local government processes and programs."

To explore the expansion idea further, the team and donor staff, with additional input from Ms. Zhang Lanying (then the China program coordinator of the International Institute for Rural Reconstruction), designed an evaluation method and invited women and men from six villages and government staff to take part in the exercise. In addition, the team carried out a self-assessment. We are currently (at the end of 2001) elaborating a new action research project proposal that builds on the results of this evaluation. In this new project we aim to design, try out and assess various mechanisms and processes (spearheaded by farmers, government staff and extensionists, and facilitated by the research team) to scale out/up our CBNRM methodology and lessons learned.

Assessment of village performance

The six villages taking part in the GAAS Community-based Natural Resource Management project usually carried out an annual assessment of their year's work and identified and rewarded good performance. Toward the end of the year, the project team would call a meeting, inviting farmer representatives

· 124 ·

(both men and women), all village leaders, and usually township leaders. At these meetings, each village group would present a summary of their achievements, their experiences, and the lessons they learned. Then, they would define a number of criteria for assessing village performance. This activity was aimed at encouraging the farmers and village leaders to participate actively in the project.

On 18 December 2000, the annual assessment meeting took place in the newly built social activity room in Dabuyang village. Twenty farmers (14 male, 6 female) and 13 village leaders (7 male, 6 female) were invited. Ms Zhang Lanying from the International Institute of Rural Reconstruction and six project researchers participated. The researchers were Chen Deshou, Sun Qiu, Xia Yuan, Yi Dixin, Li Yurong and Pan Jiawen. Although the meeting began at 9: 00 a.m. to allow farmers from Dongkou and Xiaozhai villages time to get there, most farmers arrived early. Representatives from each village gave a 10 – 15 minute presentation on their achievements, the process, and the difficulties they had encountered.

Chaoshan: The village leader gave an impressive presentation, explaining that over the past year the village had had no conflicts over forest management, distribution of irrigation water, collection of fees for drinking water, or other village affairs. He proudly summarized their achievements: "We have transparency in our management systems for the village fund, management groups, and the formulation and enforcement of rules. We report about our village fund every 3 months. The regulations were discussed and revised by most farmers, both men and women. Our management group members were selected by the farmers in the village assembly. Everybody in the village understands the management regulations and follows the regulations. We have sensed the power of participation."

That year, a women's group had been formed in Chaoshan village. Its leader also gave a brief presentation. So far, more than 30 women had participated in the activities of this volunteer group. The leader summed up what they had learned: "We gain knowledge and share experiences with each other about strawberry planting, livestock disease, fruit production, selling farm products, and other things. We make more money than before. Our words are taken into account in the family and in the village."

Guntang: A representative of Guntang village reported that they had applied the lessons they had learned before and had contributed labour, local materials (stone and sand), and money toward building a new village road. As a result, the number of motorcycles in the village had increased from 4 to 30. The village also had a forest management system that prevented people from damaging the forest.

Dabuyang: A woman from Dabuyang village reported, "Our women's group continues to collectively take care of the livestock's grazing. This helps us to save labour and to reduce conflicts caused by cattle or buffalo eating crops in the field. We clean our village regularly. Regarding forestland management, there is no further deforestation and major conflicts have not occurred since we have employed the household responsibility system starting in 1996. In this system, we have clear land boundaries, and clear responsibility, authority, and benefit distribution over the forest. Our drinking water system and irrigation facility function well. However, we encounter difficulty in water fee collection because we did not implement our regulations of water management properly and lack understanding and support from some households. We will have a village assembly soon to discuss this issue and find way to solve this problem. Our peach trees grow well and we had a good harvest this year. So, our income has increased."

Niuanyin: The Niuanyin representative explained that they had elected a new village leader. The former one had not been willing to take responsibility or spend time working for the common good of the village. Villagers had adopted a group responsibility system to manage forests and wasteland and to clarify rights, responsibilities, and benefits. They had encouraged farmers to plant trees, and, in the previous year, more than 20 000 trees had been planted on wasteland, with a survival rate as high as 94%. They had also installed a drinking water system, but unfortunately the water source was insufficient. The village representative concluded, "We learned that when we make a decision, we have to be careful and consider different aspects of things. Now, we can make decisions but we need to learn how to make good decisions."

Dongkou: The Dongkou speaker reported that, with the support (seed money, facilitation, training) of the GAAS team, the villagers had improved management regulations concerning forest and wastelands. Farmers now had an incentive to plant trees and establish an orchard. The previous year, villagers planted a total of 400 mu of trees and established a 40 mu orchard. They contributed labour, materials (available locally), and some of the funds needed to build a drinking water system, mountain ponds, and a village road. Regulations had been established for the management of these facilities and management staff had been selected by the farmers. Now it was safe to drink water, and families had enough food to meet their needs all year round. Village leaders were responsible, and there was transparency in village affairs.

Xiaozhai: The Xiaozhai village representative reported: "We did not do much work this year. We had a good harvest of peaches and sold them for a good price. We need to improve transparency in managing the village fund, otherwise we cannot solve the problem about water fee collection."

After these thoughtful and frank presentations, a short period of relaxation served to enliven the atmosphere. Zhang Lanying, who had been asked to help facilitate the meeting, organized a game followed by singing.

The participants from the six villages then defined criteria for performance assessment and rated each village accordingly (Table 21). Chaoshan village was rated highest, Dongkou second, and Dabuyang third. Most of the villagers and leaders were enthusiastic and warmly applauded the "winners." After a short break, the team began the project evaluation activity, which is included in the discussion below.

Table 21. Assessment of village performance based on farmer-established criteria (average scores)

Criteria	Chaoshan	Guntang	Dabuyang	Niuanyin	Dongkou	Xiaozhai
Local rules and enforcement	9.0	8.0	8.0	8.5	9.5	7.0
Organization of villagers	9.5	8.0	8.5	9.0	9.5	8.0
No. of projects and effectiveness	9.5	7.5	10	8.5	10	9.0
Unity of villagers	9.0	8.0	7.5	9.0	9.5	8.0
Skills gained	9.5	8.0	9.5	8.5	9.0	8.0
Women's participation	10	8.5	10	9.0	8.5	8.0
Total average score	56.5	48.0	53.5	52.5	56.0	48.0
Ranking	1	5	3	4	2	5

Note: 1 – 5 poor, 6 – 7.5 fair, 8 – 9 good, and 9.5 – 10 very good

Participatory evaluation of the GAAS project at the community level

To review the achievements and lessons learned over the past 6 years, the project team and the local farmers carried out a number of participatory evaluation activities at the meeting described above (18 December 2000) and on 3 and 4 January 2001. These are summarized in Table 22.

Before these sessions, the project researchers (assisted by Ms Zhang Lanying) prepared by discussing the key issues in terms of the "magic wheel" questions — why, what, when, where, and who — and assigning tasks. They also formulated questions to ask and identified methods for eliciting responses. Taking into account the educational level of the villagers, the team selected simple methods that do not require much writing, such as group discussion, informal sharing, and ranking.

To find out how much the villagers understood about the purpose of the CBNRM project, what changes the project has made, and what strategies have been effective, five questions were formulated:

- What is the project for?
- What interventions are the most effective in your village?
- What benefits resulted from the effective interventions?
- What is the least effective intervention in your village? Why?

Table 22. Participatory project evaluation meetings — when, where, and who

Activity	Date	Location	Participants				
			Total	Gov't officials	Village leaders	Vill-agers	Resea-rchers
Evaluation meeting with villagers and leaders of 6 participating villages	18 Dec 2000	Dabuyang meeting room	40(25men; 15women)	0	13	20	7
Evaluation meeting with Dongkou and Xiaozhai villagers	3 Jan 2001	Household in Dongkou village	21(12men; 9 women)	2	2	14	3
Evaluation meeting with Dabuyang, Chaoshan, and Niuanyin villagers	4 Jan 2001	Household in Chaoshan village	22(11men; 11women)	1	6	12	3
Evaluation meeting with non-project villagers	4 Jan 2001	Household in Chaobai village	20(11men; 9 women)	1	4	12	3

- What experience would you like to share with other villagers outside the project area?

This evaluation activity was very experimental; none of the researchers had any prior experience in carrying out such a task. Thus, after the December 2000 meeting, the team took time to reflect. They shared what they thought about the meeting, and what should be improved for the next evaluation meetings in terms of timing, tools, questions asked, and facilitation skills. To involve more villagers and to find out more about the information obtained in the first evaluation meeting, another two rounds of meetings were planned for 3 and 4 January, involving five villages.

Because the team did not want to ask the farmers to come to the project office in winter they decide to go to the villages instead. On 3 January, Professor Chen, Li Yurong, and Sun Qiu held a meeting with farmers from Xiaozhai and Dongkou villages, which are close together. Participants were randomly chosen, i.e., farmers (men and women) who were at home that day were invited to join us. Six farmers from Xiaozhai (four men and two women) and 10 from Dongkou (five men and five women) came. A township leader who happened to be inspecting tobacco planting in the village also attended. (Because tobacco is a major revenue source of Kaizhuo township, the township government had been paying a lot of attention to its production.) The leader was new to the area, but had heard about the project and was eager to participate in the evaluation meeting because he wanted to learn more about it.

The villagers were very interested in discussing the questions the project team raised. The township leader was unused to the style in which the team conducted the evaluation meeting, which was much more informal than conventional meetings and allowed the villagers to speak freely and voice their own opinions. At first, he always stood to stop farmers from speaking and he asked the villagers to be quiet and listen to the project team. The team had to explain that they wanted to know how the villagers saw the project because they were the direct beneficiaries of the project and knew more about it than anyone else.

Before the end of the meeting, the team added an additional question: which government agency was most helpful to the development of the village? Most of the farmers admitted that the township government was most helpful, because it was closest to them in terms of physical distance and administration. However, the farmers also pointed out deficiencies of the township government in helping farmers in such areas as assuring safe drinking water, fairness in tobacco collection, and ignorance about farmers' needs for good quality seeds and fertilizers, farming technology, etc. The young official was very embarrassed to hear this. After the meeting, he said that he had not realized farmers were dissatisfied with the work done by the government. He also said he would come to the villages more often to understand farmers' situation better and respond to their needs more quickly.

In the morning of 4 January, Professor Chen, Li Yurong, and Sun Qiu went to Chaoshan village to hold another evaluation meeting. The total number of farmers participating was 22, 10 from Chaoshan (including five women), six from Dabuyang (three women), and six from Niuanyin (three women). A retired township leader, who lives in Chaoshan and is respected by the villagers, also participated in the meeting, which was held in his son's house. Many people in these three villages are related through inter-village marriages, and some of the participants knew each other well.

The results of these three meetings with participating villagers are summarized below.

Question 1: What is the project for?

The answers given by the three groups of farmers were quite similar:

- For ourselves, not for others
- For better use of natural resources, for a better life of our children and grandchildren
- For village development and a better life
- For not being poor anymore, reducing poverty
- For improving knowledge and skills
- For increasing our income [mentioned frequently by the women]
- For maintaining green mountains and clean water for our children and grandchildren
- For improving living conditions
- For saving women's time for fetching water, so we have time to engage

in economic activities and having some more rest [mentioned frequently by the women]

- For strengthening villagers' solidarity through collective activities (road construction and management, management of drinking and irrigation water, collective cattle-grazing management) [mentioned frequently by women]
- For improving our skills in organization, management, and others
- For providing irrigation water for rice paddies, reducing costs, and increasing rice yield

From these benefits, it was apparent that

- The participants viewed themselves as beneficiaries, not IDRC or the research team; the villagers were motivated to realize their own goals.
- They perceived the goals of the project to be improving livelihood and production conditions, increasing income, alleviating poverty, and having a better life (getting benefits). And they thought that women had enjoyed substantial benefits.
- The project had future benefits - creating a sound environment, sustainable development, providing better conditions for future generations.
- The project built capacity (technology and management).

Question 2: What interventions are the most effective in your village?

This question was discussed in small groups organized by village. Farmers listed all the interventions in their village, then chose the two or three that they considered to have been the most effective (Table 23).

From Table 23, it is clear that the interventions the farmers ranked most highly were closely related to those that helped them earn a living: installation of potable water and irrigation facilities and road construction. Reforestation and fruit tree planting were also considered effective in terms of improving the

· 132 ·

environment and generating income. Women's groups began to play an active role in the villages. The organization of women was another effective intervention that was very much appreciated by the women. All of the interventions listed as most effective by the farmers share some common elements: active participation of farmers in decision – making and implementation; and the emphasis on the clarification of rights, obligations, responsibilities, and benefits in establishment of the management system.

Table 23. The most effective project interventions, by village

Village	Intervention	Strategies
Chaoshan	Road construction and management	Design, funds and labour inputs from the community Group responsibility Regular maintenance
	Potable water and irrigation station, installation and management	Design, construction, labour, and part of funds contributed by community Pay for use, maintenance and management, and services
	Women's learning group	Organized by village women's committee Voluntary participation Learn about animal raising, farming technology, and other skills
Guntang	Road construction and management	Labour and some funds from the community Design and construction by community Group responsibility Pay for use, maintenance, and management
Dabuyang	Potable water and irrigation station, installation and management	Design, installation, and labour contribution from community Formulating and implementing management system based on local regulations Pay for use, maintenance and management, and service
	Fruit tree planting on wasteland	Voluntarily contribute land, but individual household responsibility system Technical training Appropriate management
	Collective grazing of cattle, women's group	Voluntarily organized by women, with free participation Grazing cattle by shift, three households (usually women) per day Setting up regulations

Table 23 concluded

Village	Intervention	Strategies
Niuanyin	Irrigation facility, installation and management	Funds and labour from the community Self-design and installation Establishment of rules and regulations for effective management
	Reforestation	Free household grouping and clarifying responsibilities and benefits Good plant quality Establishment of management system
Dongkou	Reforestation	Household responsibility Clarify responsibility, authority, and benefits Establishment of management system
	Orchard establishment on wasteland and management	Voluntarily contribute land Individual household responsibility for planting Technical training Farmer-to-farmer learning
Xiaozhai	Potable water, installation and management	Labour and some funds from the community Establish regulations based on local rules Pay for use, maintenance and management, service
	Orchard establishment on wasteland	Voluntarily contribute land Individual household planting On-farm technical training Farmer-to-farmer learning Funds and labour contributed by community Democratic process
	Potable water, installation and management	Election of management personnel Establishment of management system Pay for use and management

Question 3: What benefits resulted from the effective interventions?

The answers to this question from the three groups of farmers were also quite similar. In the first round of evaluation, the project team asked participants to rank the benefits they had listed, but the farmers found this difficult. They said that all the benefits were important and most were interrelated. The effective interventions brought the following benefits to the local farmers:

- Increased crop yields and increased income [mentioned frequently by women]
- The use and management of natural resources in a sustainable manner
- Saved labour and convenience [mentioned frequently by women]
- Improved living conditions
- Conserved soil and water resources, better environment
- Improved technical skills and management capacity

The farmers have benefited from the effective interventions in several ways. Their livelihood has improved through increased crop yields and income. Their quality of life has improved in terms of better living conditions and more leisure time. And they have a sounder environment as a result of enhanced technical skills and management capacity, key components in the sustainable management of natural resources.

Question 4: What is the least effective intervention in your fvillage? Why?

When these questions were asked at the first evaluation meeting, the project team was afraid that the farmers would not want to answer them. However, the farmers had a lively discussion and provided frank answers. The team was happy to note that it had gained their trust. The responses from the various villages are listed in Table 24.

The intervention thought to be least effective differed among the villages. From these responses, the team learned that the least effective interventions are those that do not meet farmers' needs or interests, lack a clear management strategy, fail to carry out an adequate feasibility study, and lack necessary support from the outside.

Table 24. The least successful intervention, by village

Village	Intervention	Why/Reasons
Chaoshan	Irrigation station	Inadequate irrigation system, lack of fund contribution from the community
Guntang	Orchard establishment	Not coordinated, lack of management strategies
Dabuyang	Social activity room	Not urgently needed by the farmers, no incentive to contribute labour and other resources
Niuanyin	Potable water	Water source insufficient due to inadequate feasibility study
Dongkou	Construction of large pond	Leaking problem not solved, need for technical support
Xiaozhai	Raising black goats	Insufficient land for grazing; goats destroy crops which results in conflicts in the village

Question 5: What experience would you like to share with other farmers outside the project area?

The participants identified experiences they would like to share with others, then voted for the three they thought were most valuable.

Table 25. Experiences to share with others

Experience	Voting	Ranking
Unification of the community and dependence on farmers	16	1
Establishment of management system and strict enforcement of the rules	15	2
Contribution of funds and labour collectively by community	13	3
Women's active roles in natural resource management	11	4
Organizing and tasking, clear responsibility to improve management efficiency and effectiveness	7	5
Village leaders' unity and their strong sense of responsibility	6	6

Note: These results are from the third evaluation meeting only.

Farmers' participation and their unity in collective action are fundamental elements of CBNRM, and were ranked first by the farmers. We believe that the participatory planning and implementation process used in the CBNRM project created an awareness among the farmers of the power of participation. Building management institutions is another important element of CBNRM that ensures the fair use and regulation of natural resources. The strategies used in the project were setting up management groups, democratically selecting management staff, and formulating rules and regulations that were based on traditional laws. The third most important experience identified by the farmers was mobilization of community resources to increase farmers' accountability. As a Buyi farmer expressed in a folk song, "If the money is not from my pocket I may not care to make good use of it." We also learned that women play increasingly important roles in natural resource management when they are given opportunities to participate effectively.

Project evaluation in non-participating communities

Because the team wanted to expand the project beyond the six villages, they decided to find out whether farmers in neighbouring villages had learned anything about their results and approach. They organized an evaluation meeting in two non-project villages, Chaobai aud Napeng. Chaobai is on the border of the project region and has a total of 106 households, mainly of the Buyi ethnic group. Napeng is 4 – 5 km from the project region and has 53 households, mainly Han.

In the afternoon of 4 January, Professor Chen, Li Yurong, and Sun Qiu held a meeting at the home of the village leader in Chaobai. This young man, who had middle-school education, had been village leader for 4 years and had just married the woman who had been the project team's cook for the last 5 years. He had heard about the project from his wife and other sources, was interested in it, and wanted to try the CBNRM approach in his own village. He had met and talked to the project team at various times. His interest was the main reason the team had decided to hold the evaluation meeting in Chaobai.

Napeng village had also expressed an interest in the project. Most of its residents wanted to participate and had recently elected leaders who shared this interest. The village leaders and some villagers had visited the project site. Thus, farmers in the two villages were serious about the meeting.

In total, there were 16 participants, nine from Chaobai (three women) and seven from Napeng (four women), including a respected elder from Chaobai. Professor Chen introduced the project team and explained the purpose of the evaluation. The evaluation itself was conducted using discussion and some simple scoring tools. Sun Qiu acted as facilitator, raising questions and guiding the discussion; Li Yurong recorded what the participants said on a big piece of paper, which was mounted on the wall. Three questions were asked.

Question 1: How did you learn about the project?

The participants listed all the sources from which they had obtained information about the project, then ranked them in terms of importance (each participant could vote for two sources but, as the totals indicate, some participants only voted for one source). The ranking exercise was done separately by men and women (Table 26). Because some participants could not read, Li Yurong read

Table 26. Sources of information about the GAAS project listed by villagers from Napeng and Chaobai

Information source	Men's voting	Women's voting
Social chatting and interaction, especially while visiting friends and relatives in the project area	3	3
Information gained at the local market	3	2
Visit to the project villages	2	1
Television program about the project	2	1
Radio broadcast	1	1
Attendance at township meetings	1	0

the sources aloud one by one, allowing participants to respond to each. However, this made some of the women too shy to speak up. To overcome this problem in subsequent activities, the team used simple, visual tools as much as possible.

The results showed that social interactions and the local market were the most important sources of information for both women and men. Men tended to watch more and learn more from television programs. No female participant had been to a township meeting. The team concluded that farmer-to-farmer interactions seemed a very effective way to disseminate information.

Question 2: Do you know what interventions and strategies were used in the project villages?

This question was discussed in plenary. Each participant was asked to mention one intervention that he or she knew about and explain (if known) how this intervention was implemented (Table 27).

From these answers, the project team deduced that these neighbouring villagers had a lot of knowledge about the CBNRM project. They were aware of the changes in the project area and were anxious to learn more about how they had been brought about. As one farmer explained, "We are confident to achieve what the project villages have achieved." However, the team also noted that they tended to know more about the visible interventions than about those involving governance innovations, such as the establishment of management systems and the formation of management groups.

Question 3: What do you want to learn from the six villages for your own village development and better natural resource management?

The participants listed many things they wanted to learn, then organized them into seven groups. They were asked to vote for the three things they most

Table 27. GAAS project interventions that were best known to farmers in Napeng and Chaobai

Intervention	How was the intervention implemented?
Orchard establishment and management	Household responsibility system; good quality of seedlings; contribution of fertilizer and labour from households; learning by training and doing
Road construction and management	Funds and labour contributed by community; each household contributed labour; establishment of management system; payment for maintenance of the road
Establishment of high-quality rice production	Introductory trial of rice variety on farmers' fields; linking rice company with the villages to collect rice products
Potable water installation and management	Funds and labour contributed by village; constructed by themselves; installation of water-meters; payment for use, maintenance, management, and services
Reforestation	Household responsibility system; clarified responsibilities, authority, and benefits; learning technical skills for planting
Irrigation facility building and management	Labour contribution; setting up management system; reducing conflicts through the enforcement of rules
Agricultural technology dissemination	Training of farmer trainers
Cultural and educational support	Establishing a broadcasting station; improving environmental sanitation (weekly clean-up of the village); improving living conditions (rebuilding toilets)

wanted to learn about (Table 28). Note: in this exercise, votes were not segregated by sex.

The villagers wanted to learn most about the democratic election of responsible village leaders, building management systems, creating unity, and encouraging active participation. Their answers reflect their perception that leadership and community institution-building, together with villagers'active participation, are critical in community development and natural resource management. They confirm our own understanding that these are key elements for a successful CBNRM approach.

Table 28. GAAS project activities that Napeng and Chaobai villagers wanted to learn about most

Project activity	No. votes	Ranking
Democratic election of responsible village leaders	13	1
Establishing a management system	10	2
Unity of villagers and active participation	9	3
Contribution of funds and labour, collective action for natural resource management	8	4
Planting trees on waste land	6	5
Transparency in village fund management	2	6
Care for the long term benefits	1	7

After the team had reviewed the results from question 3, they asked: Would you now be able to try out these activities in your own villages? One farmer from Napeng replied, "We have tried to do what we can. We have re-elected our village leaders, organized farmers to discuss management systems for better forest management. To increase villagers' participation we need to start from the things they are mostly interested in, which are usually closely related to their livelihood improvement, such as safe drinking water, irrigation facility, taking advantage of abandoned wasteland for income generation activities. We have the manpower and materials available in the village, a little bit of money, and enthusiasm to undertake the activities, but we lack market information, seed money, technical skills, and the capacity to organize and manage. So we need support from the project and local government."

Reflection at the project team level

The second component of the project evaluation consisted of self-assessment by the project team. Three opportunities for such reflection occurred, involving various team members.

- On 31 October 2000, Chen Deshou, Sun Qiu, Xia Yuan, and Li

Zhinan met in the meeting room of Information Institute of GAAS.

- On 18 and 19 November 2000, Sun Qiu, Zhou Pidong, and Yuan Juanwen (with facilitation by Zhang Lanying) met at the University of the Philippines at Los Banos (the three team members were in the Philippines for studies at that time).
- From 19 to 21 December 2000, Chen Deshou, Sun Qiu, Xia Yuan, Pan Jiawen, Yin Dixin, and Li Yurong (with facilitation by Zhang Lanying) met in the project office in Kaizhuo township.

During these critical reviews, the team members focused on the evaluation questions defined according to suggestions made by the Ford Foundation and IDRC program officers: What have we achieved? How have the achievements been realized? What elements of CBNRM made this project successful? What lessons did we learn from our experience?

What elements of CBNRM made this project successful?

Based on the team's experience over the 6 years of the project, five important elements of CBNRM were identified as important:

- Institutionalizing sustainable natural resource management with emphasis on promoting indigenous institutions
- Integrating improvement in the villagers' livelihood and innovative management processes into the project
- Building the capacity of the local community to participate
- Encouraging women's participation in natural resource management
- Carrying out PM&E of the project process

What lessons did we learn from our experience?

The team's experience in this project allowed them to formulate some guiding principles for participatory action research:

- Respect local people
- Respect indigenous knowledge

What have we achieved? How have the achievements been realized?

Project achievement	How did this come about?	Output or outcome
Promotion of participation	Participatory project planning: • Participatory social, economic, and ecological assessment • Participatory identification of interventions and their implementation	• Villagers' initiatives • Increased unity in the community • Sense of ownership • Sense of responsibility
Financial management	Contribution of funds and labour: • Participation of local community in the form of funding and labour to construct infrastructure with limited investment of external funds • The community was involved in decisions about infrastructure projects • Funds were managed together by project team and local community, for purchases and in terms of accounting • Cash flow properly managed • Adaptation of existing financial management practices	• More unity in the community • Concern for social welfare • Sense of ownership • Sense of responsibility • Changed behaviour regarding dependence on external funds
Establishment of management systems	Management systems were: • Built on existing village regulations and traditional practices regarding the management of natural resources • Participatory approach in developing the management system • Democratic election of village leaders • Established mechanism for payments (pay-for-use fee), and for management of costs and services • Collective voting for natural resources management systems • Education through traditional folk songs	• Emerging women leaders • Management capability to take care of more projects • Proper management of natural resources • Improved ecological conditions on farms • Capability in planting diversified crops
Capacity enhancement	Capacity-building focused on: • Enhancing the ability of villagers to participate (knowledge about technologies and organization and management skills) • Enhancing skills in terms of utilization and decision-making, e.g., water pricing • Enhancing management skills (developing new and revising existing systems)	• Attitude change toward participation • Ensured sustainability of the project • Ensured sustainability of natural resource use

- Meeting local people's needs is the critical factor in achieving their active participation
- Understand fully the real needs of local people
- Integrate people's needs into the broader development of the area
- Make participatory investment a part of projects

Project evaluation at the government level

Looking to the future and the possibility of expanding the project, it was also important to get a clear understanding of government officials' knowledge about the approach and methods of CBNRM in general and the GAAS project in particular. Discussions were held with the following officials:

- Officials of the Foreign Fund Management Centre under the Provincial Poverty Alleviation Office (18 January 2001)
- Directors of the Project Planning Division and the Integrated Development Division of the Provincial Poverty Alleviation Office (22 January 2001)
- A vice-county leader from Fenggan county (25 January 2001)
- The vice-mayor of Qiannan Prefecture, who is in charge of agricultural development (3 February 2001)

In these meetings, the project team usually briefly presented the project objectives, interventions, methods, outputs, and impacts, then invited the officials to comment. This was followed by a discussion of more specific topics: farmers' participation in decision-making; establishment of CBNRM systems focusing on local institution-building; and improving the capacities of local communities.

Farmers' participation in decision-making : This is still a new concept to most government officials in China, who are used to top-down thinking and decision-making. They see themselves as the planners; they make decisions. One official mentioned the lack of trust in farmers' ability to make decisions; therefore, government imposes ideas on them. He added that this attitude gives farmers no incentive to do what government wants them to do, and sometimes even creates hostility toward the government. Another official observed that if farmers participated in decision-making, the decisions would reflect farmers' interests, meet their needs, and benefit them. They would perceive the project as theirs and the work would be for themselves rather than to achieve the government's goals. Other officials commented that, in the GAAS project, it was apparent that each decision was made with the whole village involved, and thus the issues became truly those of the village (not the government). They concluded that this had generated the high level of commitment and responsibility shown by the farmers.

Establishment of CBNRM systems focusing on local institution-building: The officials of the Foreign Fund Management Centre were interested in the establishment of farmer groups for natural resource management. During implementation of the GAAS project, various management groups had been set up, such as the women's cattle-grazing group in Dabuyang, the women's learning group in Chaoshan, forest management groups in various villages, and management groups for the irrigation systems. The formulation of rules and regulations had involved most of the farmers in each village, and their enforcement had been successful to date. The officials realized that this community – based mechanism could ensure the sustainable use and management of the natural resources. They concluded that a distinctive characteristic of the GAAS project had been its focus on strengthening community-based management systems and establishing the farmer groups.

Improving the capacities of local communities: The officials all agreed that the capacity of farmers needed to be enhanced if CBNRM systems were to be successful. During the discussion, they particularly mentioned the need for farmers to know more about community organization, leadership, communications, marketing, the adoption and adaptation of farming technologies, and the sustainable use of resources. One of the directors pointed out that failure to train farmers would limit their participation. But he noted that training is only one of the ways to improve farmers' abilities; fieldwork is even more important. He observed that the GAAS project had done well in this respect. However, he also commented that the project was weak in terms of giving farmers more opportunities to get information and make use of public services. In his view, having access to more information would mean a broader perspective, which would lead to wiser decision-making.

Synthesis

In reviewing the assessments of project achievements and future challenges made by selected villagers, government officials, and research team members, we observe many commonalities. The key elements for success that were identified at the project team level (participatory planning, management-system development through a participatory approach, capacity-building) match the views expressed by community members and government officials. These, in turn, validate the assumptions that we had made about the central elements of our CBNRM approach and methods. The factors cited most often are:

- Capacity - building for participation (confidence building, leadership, management, organization)
- Institution - building for sustainable natural resource management with emphasis on promoting indigenous institutions
- Integrating both livelihood improvement and innovative management processes into projects
- Increasing women's participation in natural resource management
- Integrating participatory monitoring and evaluation into the project cycle

To these, we would like to add the importance of good relations and mutual trust between project staff and the local communities, and between project staff and government staff. Although this element did not emerge explicitly during the assessment exercises, we consider it worthwhile highlighting.

    The GAAS project involved the participation of the local people in a variety of ways. As a result, the communities have a very strong sense of ownership and accountability. They participated in the projects "for themselves, not for others." And they have been trying to "fulfill their life dreams." These statements reveal the impact that the villagers' ability to participate has had on their attitudes. They are more determined than ever, and are headed toward their own self-development. Community people, especially women, were empowered through capacity-building and participation in the election of village leaders, in the establishment of their fair and equal rights in natural resource management, in decisions about their future, and in the implementation and continuation of the projects. Through collective action, they are more united and more confident about solving their own problems.

6. Making room for change: progress and challenges

The chapters of this book document how we integrated a PM&E process into ongoing field research at selected sites in Yunnan and Guizhou. In this chapter, we build on the reflections of the individual teams presented in chapters 3 – 5. We look back at the key elements of the training and fieldwork process and assess the value that the PM&E work added as well as the highlights and shortcomings of the process. We also look to the future and outline ideas for continuing and strengthening the work that we began.

Two decades' of rapid economic growth have taught Chinese leaders and the public an important lesson: economic growth shall not be achieved at the cost of environmental and ecological destruction. High on the list of national priorities are environmental protection and sustainable development. Transition from a command-and-control system to a market-oriented economy requires that new instruments and incentives, institutional strategies, and mechanisms be explored, experimented with, and adapted to local contexts. A large number of government policies and regulations have been established to support this transition; at the same time, bold initiatives of villagers are bringing about new forms of local change, slowly but remarkably (as we have documented in this book). As a result, the relations among the various stakeholders are also changing. Government agencies must deal with more diverse and vocal clients than during the commune era when it was already difficult to address the diversity of needs and problems. In Yunnan and Guizhou a number of government officials have taken up this new challenge. Small farmers and indigenous people who feel the need for institutional change are developing innovative collective methods to improve their livelihood and achieve a more sustainable future. PM&E is one of the elements contributing to these changes.

The value of PM&E

Learning about PM&E and applying the concepts and tools in our *particular* local contexts has been a challenging, demanding, but worthwhile enterprise. PM&E opened a new window on our research practice. Its integration into the project cycle has strengthened the learning, accountability, and effectiveness of the two research teams and their work, in particular through the discovery that what matters is not only *what* is assessed, but also *who* does the assessing. We have learned that it is important to make careful decisions about whose voices and insights we take into account when determining research progress and achievements and when looking at new challenges and opportunities. PM&E has allowed us to bring the various people with whom we are working—the women and men in the villages and in government offices in particular—closer to each other. It has given all of us a better understanding of each other's points of view, interests, doubts, and desires.

The experience has also contributed to a better understanding of *how* the various concerns and interests of villagers (both men and women), government officials and researchers are represented and negotiated in a research process. We now better understand that carrying out research is a social process. We are more aware that negotiations, tensions, and unintended consequences are parts of the puzzle of doing research and PM&E. As the two case studies prove, the training and fieldwork in particular contributed greatly to a better understanding by researchers and local government officials of the interests and needs of farmers. Our experience confirms, as Guijt et al. (1998) have suggested, that putting PM&E on our agenda is a journey and not a destination. Our journey continues.

At the third training workshop in Baoshan (May – June 2001), the project teams summarized the added value of the PM&E work:

- More trust in each other (researchers, farmers, government officials) and a recognition of each other's roles, strengths and weaknesses
- Increased understanding and cooperation among stakeholders in an effort to join forces and achieve common goals
- Increased opportunities for farmers' participation, particularly women, in the research and change processes
- Farmers' increased sense of ownership of the project, both of the

process and the outcomes

- Contribution to building a stronger community identity through a variety of collective efforts
- Clearer project objectives and expected outcomes that are closer to the diversity of interests and needs of villagers
- Improved project management with more space for reflection, responsiveness, and adaptation

A balancing act: the training method and process

The training component was designed as an experimental pilot process for IDRC's Community-based Natural Resource Management program and as a complementary activity for the two research projects/teams. It is worthwhile noting that the chain of action that we had envisioned (and described in chapter 1) proved feasible and effective. The seven steps are listed again below, along with brief comments on the extent to which each was realized.

1. *Resources are devoted to monitoring and evaluation, including stakeholder time and financial inputs*: We were lucky to have access to important resources — staff, funds, transportation — that allowed us to go out into the field. Farmers and government staff also dedicated time and effort to the monitoring and evaluation work. However, how much time should be dedicated to this activity remains a thorny question.

2. *Working with intended users, important monitoring and evaluation issues and questions are defined, and, based on these, the design is prepared and data are collected*: We made considerable progress in this step, but we think that we can still improve considerably on how we jointly establish the monitoring and evaluation plans. Increasing the quality of participation remains a challenge.

3. *Key stakeholders and primary users are involved throughout the process*: As in step 2, there is room for improvement during the different stages of the research process, from the initial idea and design

stage to the actual use of the PM&E results.

4. ***Intended users react to their involvement***: We paid careful attention to this step, and overall, feedback has been very positive. However, we need to pay more attention to the possibly different ideas, viewpoints, interests, suggestions and desires that people involved have. Besides, there is a need to not forget those not directly involved or visible or vocal.

5. ***The monitoring and evaluation process and findings provide (new) knowledge and understanding***: As mentioned above, we consider that this has occurred among the various groups involved.

6. ***Intended users interpret results, generate and adopt recommendations, and use the monitoring and evaluation results***: So far, farmers in the research sites (and beyond) have done this to varying degrees. The two research teams have been able to use the results to adapt the research management process and methods on a number of occasions and we are now also exploring the use of the results beyond the project level.

7. ***The project improves and (new) decisions are made***: We consider this to be the case. We are continuing the journey.

Considering the training workshops as milestones in this chain of events we briefly reflect on what was accomplished. Going back to the beginning of the training process, the first workshop in 1999 achieved the following: a basic understanding among the stakeholders of concepts and methods, the motivation to think carefully about participation, draft monitoring and evaluation plans (using the six questions on the magic wheel), a readiness to try things out, and a set of useful training exercises. Its two major shortcomings were: language problems (facilitators, and translation of reading materials), and the exchanges between the teams could have been more intense (GAAS 1999).

About halfway through the process (after the second workshop in 2000), we identified the following progress: better understanding of what PM&E is all about (basic concepts, use of tools, and a change in attitude among the researchers); the realization that to be meaningful and useful, PM&E must be an integral part of the research process, not just an add on; the realization that there is no blueprint for PM&E (the GAAS and KIB cases differed); the importance of understanding context (previous experiences, backgrounds, and politics); and the development of a useful set of exercises. We noted several opportunities for improvement: more practice is needed; the facilitator (s) must participate in the fieldwork; successful case studies are needed to allow us to learn from experience; translation remains a constraint; defining indicators is still a problem (especially avoiding getting side-tracked by this); and how to get farmers on board is not always evident (KIB 2000).

During the third workshop, the teams reflected on the highlights of the PM&E training project as well as the major challenges. The lists resulting from the subsequent plenary session follow.

Highlights

- The magic wheel of PM&E (the six key guiding questions for doing PM&E)
- PM&E as an incentive for stakeholder participation in the research process
- The need to identify specific indicators for different stakeholders
- The involvement of the local government in the evaluation
- Research teams now have a good understanding of and attitudes for PM&E
- PM&E contributed to increased transparency in the research process

Challenges

- How to best combine conventional monitoring and evaluation with participatory monitoring and evaluation; how to combine old and new tools
- How to balance PM&E guidelines (theory) with flexibility in implementing the process in local contexts

- How to deal with the often complex social dynamics that shape the process in sometimes unforeseen ways (power relations, conflicts in communities)
- How to deal with the Chinese political (top – down) system and ingrained thinking and behaviour
- How to better involve government staff in the monitoring and evaluation process from beginning to end
- How farmers can adapt PM&E to their own situation and what role researchers should play in this process
- How to improve the facilitation of exercises and processes in the field
- How to provide ongoing training

Future steps

Both teams have been working to meet these challenges and continue the work they have begun. We are looking at strengthening access and capacities within the KIB and GAAS, as well as reaching out and collaborating with other organizations. The following "internal" steps have been suggested:

- Establish a monitoring and evaluation system at the organizational level.
- Organize more regular meetings of research (project) teams to discuss achievements and lessons learned.
- Establish monitoring and evaluation indicators for our research activities.
- Little by little , institutionalize PM&E into the project cycles of other projects managed by KIB and GAAS.
- Move from PM&E as a tool in the hands of research staff to a tool mastered by local people, so as to initiate a learning process at the local level (e.g., expand on the pilot self-monitoring experience of the farmers in the six villages in Guizhou).
- Develop new and better - adapted monitoring and evaluation tools together with local farmers.
- Further train our local government partners in designing and

implementing participatory projects.

- For the PARDYP team: Spend more time in the villages explaining our mission and project style and building local people's organizational capacity.

In cooperation with other organizations, we are exploring the following actions:

- Share experiences, for example, through conferences and workshops, field visits, networking, web pages.
- Develop and publish a PM&E manual in Chinese.
- Undertake fieldwork with various other organizations to develop monitoring and evaluation systems jointly.
- Organize training of trainers.

Despite our efforts over the last 2 years, we are still at an early stage in terms of making PM&E an operating principle. Much has been learned, but more remains to be done. Integrating PM&E into the work of any organization requires a long-term process of learning by doing, adapting, and adopting step-by-step changes. It is a process that should not be rushed nor imposed; rather, it should be allowed to take root in people's day-to-day thinking so that it eventually becomes automatic. As Norman Uphoff so aptly put it in *Learning from Gal Oya*, "this can be a rocky road, but a preferable one" (1992: 12).

Appendix 1: Programs for the three workshops

The workshop programs (below) and the exercises (Appendix 2) were designed to take into account the local context, aspirations, and experience of both research teams and their available resources. Both the programs for the workshops and the exercises evolved over time, i.e., those for the second workshop built on the results and assessment of the first workshop and the fieldwork carried out in the interval between them. The program and exercises for the third workshop were based on progress made during the second workshop and the second round of fieldwork. We include this material as *examples* with the hope that they might be useful to those planning other training initiatives, although it will likely have to be adapted to other contexts and environments.

Workshop 1, Guiyang, Guizhou province, 20 – 23 July 1999
hosted by the Guizhou Academy of Agricultural Sciences

Tuesday, 20 July
    18:00 – 20:00   Welcome diner, introduction of participants

Wednesday, 21 July
    09:00 – 10:00   Introduction and formulation of expectations (Exercise 1)
    10:00 – 11:00   Participatory monitoring and evaluation: defining the core
                     concepts (Exercise 2)
                     *Participatory monitoring and evaluation: the key
                     questions (part 1)*
    11:00 – 12:00   Why? (Exercise 3)
    12:00 – 13:30   Lunch
    13:30 – 15:00   What? (Exercise 4)

· 155 ·

15:00 – 15:30   Tea break

15:30 – 16:30   What? (continued) (Exercise 5)

Thursday July 22

Participatory monitoring and evaluation: the key questions (part 2)

09:00 – 10:00   For whom? (Exercise 6)

10:00 – 11:00   Who? (Exercise 7)

11:00 – 12:00   When? (Exercise 8)

12:00 – 13:30   Lunch

13:30 – 15:00   How? (Exercise 9)

15:00 – 15:30   Tea break

15:30 – 16:30   How? (continued)

Friday July 23

09:00 – 10:00   Data analysis, recording, and reporting.

10:00 – 11:00   Things that can happen. Questions?

11:00 – 12:00   Evaluation and review of expectations (Exercise 10)

12:00 – 13:30   Lunch

13:30 – 16:00   Proposal writing (fine – tuning)

16:00 – 17:00   Presentation of proposals and feedback

17:00 – 17:30   Closing

Notes:

- During the morning sessions, there will be a coffee break.
- At the end of each day, we will review the day's activities.

Workshop 2, Kunming, Yunnan province, 6 – 8 April 2000

hosted by the Kunming Institute of Botany

Thursday, 6 April

09:00 – 09:15   Welcome

09:15 – 10:00   Introduction to the second workshop (Exercise 1)

10:00 – 11:00	Project presentation by GAAS – Guizhou CBNRM team and feedback (Exercise 2)
11:00 – 11:30	Coffee and tea break
11:30 – 12:30	PM&E presentation by GAAS – Guizhou CBNRM team and feedback (Exercise 3)
12:30 – 14:30	Lunch
14:30 – 15:30	Project presentation by KIB – PARDYP team
15:30 – 15:45	Tea and coffee break
15:45 – 16:45	Project presentation by KIB – PARDYP team (continued) and feedback (Exercise2)
16:45 – 17:15	Preparation for the second day of the workshop

Friday, 7 April

09:00 – 09:15	Introduction to working group sessions
09:15 – 10:30	PM&E presentation by KIB – PARDYP team, and feedback (Exercise 3)
10:30 – 11:00	Coffee and tea
11:00 – 12:30	Working groups, session 1 (Exercises 4 and 5)
12:30 – 14:30	Lunch
14:30 – 16:00	Working groups, session 2 (Exercises 6 and 7)
16:00 – 16:15	Tea and coffee break
16:15 – 17:00	Planning future work and the 3rd PM&E workshop
17:00 – 17:30	Evaluation

Saturday, 8 April

| 09:00 – 12:00 | Report writing (Exercise 8) and other business |

Workshop 3, Baoshan, Yunnan province, 31 May to 2 June 2001

hosted by the Kunming Institute of Botany

Thursday 31 May

09:00 – 09:15	Welcome
09:15 – 09:30	Introduction to the 3rd workshop
09:30 – 10:30	Presentation by the GAAS team
10:30 – 11:00	Tea and coffee break
11:00 – 12:00	Presentation by the KIB team
12:00 – 14:00	Lunch break
14:00 – 15:00	Presentation by the Yunnan Maternal and Child Health Centre team
15:00 – 15:30	Tea break
15:30 – 17:00	Discussion: Main insights and lessons learned (Exercise 1)

Friday, 1 June

Field trip

Saturday, 2 June

09:00 – 10:30	Publishing the results
10:30 – 11:00	Tea and coffee break
11:00 – 12:00	Evaluation of the training project (Exercise 2)
12:00 – 14:00	Lunch and rest
14:00 – 15:00	Evaluation of the training project (continued)
15:00 – 15:30	Tea break
15:30 – 17:00	Next steps (Exercise 3)
17:00	Closing

Appendix 2: Exercises carried out at the three training workshops

Workshop 1

Exercise 1: Formulation of expectations
This exercise will be done in plenary.
30 minutes

- Please formulate what you expect from the workshop: what do you expect to learn or to get out of it? Do not hesitate to formulate more than one expectation.
- Keep your expectation(s) as we will review them at the end of the workshop.

Exercise 2: Definition of the core concepts PARTICIPATORY (PARTICIPATION), MONITORING, and EVALUATION
This exercise will be done in plenary.
45 minutes

- Please describe what the core concepts of participatory (participation), monitoring and evaluation mean. Use short descriptions or key words. Use cards.
- Please give one example of your own experience with each of these concepts or with a combination of these concepts (participatory monitoring, participatory evaluation).

Exercise 3: Defining the goals of participatory monitoring and evaluation (Why?)
Exercise (a) will be done in plenary.

15 minutes

- Please list possible goals or aims of doing participatory monitoring and evaluation in a research project. Use cards.

Exercise (b) will be done in 2 groups: the GAAS and PARDYP teams.

30 minutes

- Please turn now to your own project and list the possible goal(s) of implementing participatory monitoring and evaluation. If you have more than one goal, please try to list them in order of importance.
- Use a flipchart to list the goals.
- Select one member of the team to present to the plenary how the group did the exercise and what the results are.

Exercise 4: Defining the objectives of participatory monitoring and evaluation (What?)

This exercise will be done in 2 groups: the GAAS and PARDYP teams.

60 minutes

- Please define the possible object(s) of participatory monitoring and evaluation in your project. If you have listed more than one object, please try to rank them in order of importance. Explain the reason(s) for your selection.
- Use a flipchart to list the goals.
- Select one member of the team to present to the plenary how the group did the exercise and what the results are.

Exercise 5: The use of indicators (What?)

This exercise will be done in 2 groups: the GAAS and PARDYP teams.

45 minutes

- Translate the objectives listed in exercise 4 into clear and measurable indicators. Each objective should have at least one indicator, but feel free to list more than one.
- Suggest for each indicator how it could be measured.

- Use cards and the flipchart as you see appropriate.
- Select one member of the team (not the same as persons as in previous exercises) to present to the plenary how the group did the exercise and what the results are.

Exercise 6: Defining the "beneficiaries" of participatory monitoring and evaluation (For whom?)

This exercise will be done in 2 groups: the GAAS and PARDYP teams.

45 minutes

- Please define for each of the listed objects and related indicator(s) for whom these will be relevant. Be as specific as possible, referring to your project situation.
- Use card and the flipchart as you see appropriate.
- Select one member of the team (not the same as persons as in previous exercises) to present to the plenary how the group did the exercise and what the results are.

Exercise 7: Defining the implementers of participatory monitoring and evaluation (Who?)

This exercise will be done in 2 groups: the GAAS and PARDYP teams.

45 minutes

- Please define for each of the listed objects and related indicator(s) who will be responsible for doing the participatory and monitoring. Be as specific as possible.
- Use cards and the flipchart as you see appropriate.
- Select one member of the team to present to the plenary how the group did the exercise and what the results are.

Exercise 8: The timing of participatory monitoring and evaluation in your project (When?)

This exercise will be done in 2 groups: the GAAS and PARDYP teams.

45 minutes

- Please define a calendar for each of the listed participatory monitoring and evaluation activities defined in the exercises carried out so far.
- Use cards and the flipchart as you see appropriate.
- Select one member of the team to present to the plenary how the group did the exercise and what the results are.

Exercise 9: Selecting the tools for participatory monitoring and evaluation (How?)

Exercise (a), done in plenary.

30 minutes

Please indicate which tools you know about or have heard of that are useful for doing participatory monitoring and evaluation.

Exercise (b) will be done in the PARDYP and GAAS teams.

45 minutes

- Return to your own project. Please identify the appropriate tool(s) for each of the identified participatory monitoring and evaluation activities in your project.
- Please specify if you require additional training to use these tools.
- Use cards and the flipchart as you see appropriate.
- Select one member of the team to present to the plenary how the group did the exercise and what the results are.

Exercise 10: Evaluating the workshop

- Surprise!
- Please wait for instructions. (The group was asked to design a workshop evaluation based on what was learned including the design or selection of at least 2 tools.)

Workshop 2

Exercise 1: The meaning of PM&E

This exercise will be done in four small groups; group work will then be presented in plenary

30 minutes

- Based on your experiences to date with implementing PM&E in Yunnan and Guizhou provinces, please make a drawing of what PM&E means to you. If necessary, you could draw more than one image.
- Compare your drawing with the drawings of the other groups . Make comments.
- Do you think farmers or villagers would understand your drawing ? Why would they or why would they not?
- What happened in your small group? Why did this happen?

Excercise 2: Learning from each other

This exercise will be prepared by each team and then presented and discussed in plenary.

30 minutes

- Imagine that you are actually visiting the other research site. Please identify three "things" that you think would be useful in your own project and fieldwork. Explain why and how you would use these "things."
- What suggestions would you have for the other team to do things differently, maybe based on your own fieldwork experience? Explain why and how these changes could be implemented. Try to identify at least two changes.

Exercise 3: Reflecting on the PM&E fieldwork

This exercise will be prepared by each team and then presented and discussed in plenary.

30 minutes

- Please identify, on a card, the most important thing that you have learned from the PM&E presentation made by the other team. On another card, please write the one thing that you would like to learn more about.

- How do your cards relate to the 6 key PM&E questions (i. e. the magic wheel of PM&E)?
- Concerning the "still to learn more about" cards, are there topics that you consider more important than others?

Exercise 4: Reviewing the fieldwork: important questions

This exercise will be done in 4 small groups; results will then be presented and discussed in plenary.

45 minutes

- Based on the two PM&E presentations, four important questions have emerged. These questions are closely related to the exercise 3 as well. Please answer for both projects each of these four questions and also explain why these are "important" questions. The four questions are:

  What exactly is being monitored and evaluated and who has decided about this?

  Who is doing the monitoring and evaluation?

  How are the monitoring and evaluation done in practice? Are the two projects using the same tools?

  Now that you are implementing PM&E, has there been a change in the project? Do you see a difference?

Exercise 5: Factors shaping the process of PM&E implementation

This exercise will be done in two groups (by team); results will then be presented and compared in plenary.

45 minutes

- To better understand the implementation process of PM&E, it is important need to look at the context in which we as researchers work. Please consider the following factors that shape the process and-based on your own field experience-review them by filling in the table presented below.

Factors	Relevance	Enabling	Constraining	How to deal with factors?
Social aspects of natural resource management, such as values, norms, difference between men and women, occurrence of conflicts				
Attitudes of the researchers and their understanding of the local context				
Perceptions of the local people about the research process				
The skills of the researchers and of the local people				

Exercise 6: Decision-making in the PM&E process

This exercise will be done in two small groups (by team); results will then be presented and discussed in plenary.

45 minutes

- Participation is a central feature in the stages of the PM&E process. However, there are various ways to participate with likely, different results. Please reflect on the decision-making in your own PM&E field work by filling in the following table.

Exercise 7: Selecting indicators

This exercise will be done in two small groups (mixed). Results will be presented in plenary.

45 minutes

- As we already experienced during the 1st workshop, it is very difficult to identify indicators for the participatory monitoring and evaluation of project progress. Please review the following aspects or components of your project and identify two appropriate indicators for each of them.

At the same time, please think about how you could measure these indicators.

Research step or activity	Who controls decision-making?	Who implements the activity?	Who will benefit from the results?
Identification of research problem			
Defining the research questions			
Defining the methodology and selecting the tools			
Implementation			
Monitoring			
Evaluation			

Component	Indicator	Tool
Development		
Participation		
Communication		
Capacity development		
Learning		

Exercise 8: Writing: key questions

This exercise will be done in plenary, in the form of a brainstorming exercise.
90 minutes

- Let us imagine that we would like to write about our experiences with PM&E. In order to plan such a writing exercise, it is important to answer three questions:

  Why would we write about our experiences?

What would we write about?

For whom would we write?

Workshop 3

Exercise 1: Reflecting on the fieldwork

60 minutes

- The following are some of the major questions that allow us to reflect on the fieldwork carried out so far. Some of these questions have been addressed in the presentations. Please discuss the questions not yet addressed in your team. Please, also suggest one ore more other key reflection questions. Questions:

  1. How have you dealt with the 6 key questions for doing PM&E (the magic wheel)?

  2. How does the fieldwork carried out compare to the original PM&E plan designed during the 1st workshop? What has happened and why?

  3. What has been the added value of integrating a PM&E component into the CBNRM research projects?

  4. What have been the highlights of the PM&E fieldwork?

  5. What have been the major challenges?

  6. Who has participated in the fieldwork? In which activities?

Exercise 2: Assessing the PM&E training project methodology

90 minutes

- Please design, in a small group of volunteers, an evaluation of the PM&E training project, in particular concerning the methodology and dynamics used (i.e., process focussed). Design a variety of tools (at least 2) that can be used during the workshop.

Exercise 3: Defining possible next steps

Two mixed groups, followed by a plenary

90 minutes

- Based on the experiences and insights gained so far, are you interested in a follow up to the PM&E work? If so, define the expected results, goals and potential activities.

References

Abbot J.; Guijt I. 1998. *Changing views on change*: *participatory approaches to monitoring and evaluation*. International Institute for Environment and Development, London, UK. SARL discussion paper no. 2

Allen R.; Schreier H.; Brown, S.; Shah, P.B. eds. 2000. *The people and resource dynamics project*. *The first three years* (*1996 – 1999*). International Centre for Integrated Mountain Development, Kathmandu, Nepal.

Armonia R . C . ; Campilan D . M . 1 9 9 7 . *Participatory monitoring and evaluation*: *the Asian experience*. UPWARD, Los Banos, Laguna, Philippines.

Assessment Working Group. 1998. Final report on the participants' assessment of the Yunnan upland management (YUM) training programme. Winrock International, Asian Regional Office, Beijing, China.

Chambers R . 1993. *Challenging the professions* . Intermediate Technology Publications, London, UK.

――――――― 1997. *Whose reality counts*? *Putting the last first* . Intermediate Technology Publications, London, UK.

Chen Deshou; He Yuannong; Xia Yuan; Zhou Pidong; Sun Qiu; Li Zhinan; Yuan Juanwen; Zhao Zeying. 2000. *Community-based natural resource management in the mountainous areas of Guizhou province* , *China*. Guizhou Academy of Agricultural Sciences, Guiyang, China.

Community-Based Natural Resource Management program initiative . 2000. *CBNRM Prospectus 2000 – 2004* . International Development Research Centre, Ottawa, Canada.

Davis-Case D . 1989. *Community forestry* : *participatory assessment* , *monitoring and evaluation*. Food and Agriculture Organisation of the United Nations, Rome, Italy.

Dayal R. ; van Wijk C. ; Mukherjee N. 2000. *Methodology for participatory assessments. With communities, institutions and policy makers*. Water and Sanitation Program, the World Bank, Washington D.C., USA.

Estrella M. ; Gaventa J. 1998. *Who counts reality? Participatory monitoring and evaluation: a literature review*. Institute of Development Studies, Brighton, UK. Working paper no. 70.

Estrella M. ; Blauert J; Campilan D. ; Gaventa J. ; Gonsalves J. ; Guijt I. ; Johnson D. ; Ricafort R., eds. 2000. *Learning from change: issues and experiences in participatory monitoring and evaluation*. Intermediate Technology Publications, London, UK, and International Development Research Centre, Ottawa, Canada.

GAAS (Guizhou Academy of Agricultural Sciences). 1999. *Strengthening participatory monitoring and evaluation skills in China*. Report from the first workshop. GAAS, Guiyang, China.

Guijt I . ; ArevaloM . ; Saladores K . 1998. *Tracking change together* . International Institute for Environment and Development, London, UK. PLA notes 31: 28 – 36.

Guy S ; Inglis A. S . 1999. Tips for trainers: introducing the " H - form, " a method for monitoring and evaluation. International Institute for Environment and Development, London, UK. PLA notes 34: 84 – 87.

Johnson D . 2000. *Laying the foundation : capacity building for participatory monitoring and evaluation. In: Estrella, M.; Blauert, J; Campilan, D.; Gaventa, J.; Gonsalves, J.; Guijt, I.; Johnson, D.; Ricafort, R., eds. 2000. Learning from change: issues and experiences in participatory monitoring and evaluation*. Intermediate Technology Publications, London, UK, and International Development Research Centre, Ottawa, Canada. Pp. 217 – 228.

IUCN (International Union for Conservation of Nature and Natural Resources). 1997. *An approach to assessing progress toward sustainability-tools and training series*. Prepared by the ICUN/IDRC International Assessment Team and pilot country teams in Colombia, India and Zimbabwe. International Union for Conservation of Nature and Natural Resources,

Gland, Switzerland and Cambridge, UK.

Kristof N. D. ; WuDunn S. 2000. *Thunder from the east : portrait of a rising Asia*. Alfred A. Knopf, New York, USA.

KIB (Kunming Institute of Botany). 2000. *Strengthening participatory monitoring and evaluation skills in China*. Report from the second workshop. KIB, Kunming, China.

Li Xiaoyun, ed. 2001. *Participatory development. Theories , methods , tools*. Beijing Agricultural University, Beijing, China.

Long N. ; Long A. eds. 1992. Battlefields of knowledge: the interlocking of theory and practice in social research and development. Routledge, London, UK.

Lu Xing, 2000. *Searching for participatory approaches : findings of the Yunnan PRA network*. International Institute for Environment and Development, London, UK. PLA notes 37: 4 – 8.

Margoluis R. ; Salafsky N. 1998. *Measures of success : designing , managing , and monitoring conservation and development projects*. Island Press, Washington D.C. and Covelo, CA, USA.

McAllister K. 1999. Understanding participation : monitoring and evaluation process, outputs and outcomes. International Development Research Centre, Ottawa, Canada. Research paper.

McAllister K. ; Vernooy R. 1999. *Action and reflection : a guide for monitoring and evaluation*. International Development Research Centre, Ottawa, Canada.

Patton M. Q. 1978, 1997. *Utilization - focused evaluation*. Sage Publications, Thousand Oaks, USA, London, UK, and New Delhi, India.

Pretty J. 1995. Participatory learning for sustainable agriculture , World Development, 23(8): 1247 – 1264.

Rigg J. 1997. Souheast Asia. Routledge, London, UK.

Robinson S. A. ; Cox P. ; Somlai I. G. ; Prasai B. R. 1997. Process evaluation: a field method for tracking those elusive development results. *Canadian Journal of Development Studies* , 18: 805 – 834.

Sun Qiu; Zhou Pidong; Vernooy, R. 2000. *The role of participatory monitoring and evaluation*. Presented at the 2nd International Community-Based Natural Resource Management Workshop, Guiyang, 16 – 20 October 2000. International Development Research Centre, Ottawa, Canada.

Uphoff N. 1992. Learning from Gal Oya. Cornell University Press, Ithaca, USA, and London, UK.

Vernooy, R. 2001. *Connected*: *insights from the 2nd International Community-based Natural Resource Management workshop*. International Development Research Centre, Ottawa, Canada.

Wilkes A. 2000. *What can participation really do? Summary report on findings of project – based reflections on PRA in South West China*. Kunming, *China*. Yunnan PRA Network, Kunming, China. Unpublished paper.

About the editors

Xu Jianchu is executive director of the Centre for Biodiversity and Indigenous Knowledge. He holds a PhD in environmental resource management from the China Agricultural University and has extensive field experience in southwest China and the greater Mekong region in the areas of ethnobotany, indigenous knowledge, biodiversity conservation, and participatory technology development. Dr Jianchu is a member of the boards of the Regional Community Forestry Training Centre for Asia and the Pacific and the International Society of Ethnobiology. He also sits on the steering committee for Land-Use and Land-Cover Change of the International Geosphere-Biosphere Global Change Program. Currently, he is coordinating projects on ethnobotanical inventories, biodiversity conservation, community-based natural resource management, watershed management, and ecosystem rehabilitation. He is author of five published monographs and 50 scientific papers.

Sun Qiu has a master's degree in social development from Ateneo De Manila University in the Philippines. She is a senior researcher and the director of the Integrated Rural Development Centre at the Guizhou Academy of Agricultural Sciences. She was a core team member of the IDRC-funded project "Community-based Natural Resource Management in Mountainous Areas of Guizhou Province" Phases I and II (1995 – 2001). Sun Qiu has extensive experience in community-based natural resource management and in rural development research. She is a member of the group that coordinates the recently established Farmer-centered Research/ Community-based Natural Resource Management Network in China.

Ronnie Vernooy is a senior program specialist at the International Development Research Centre, Ottawa, Canada. He received his PhD in the sociology of rural development from the Agricultural University of Wageningen (Holland) in 1992 and joined IDRC the same year. His research interests include rural development, natural resource management, agricultural biodiversity, and participatory (action) research methods including monitoring and evaluation. His current work focuses on Southeast Asia (China and Viet Nam), Central America, and Cuba; he has a special interest in Nicaragua where he carried out field research in both hillside and coastal environments during 1985 – 86, 1988 – 91 and 1997 – 98. His first visit to China (Yunnan and Guizhou provinces) took place in early 1999. Fascinated by the diversity and dynamism of the Chinese people, he has returned on several occasions to learn more about the changes brought about by the women and men there, especially in rural areas. Recent publications include *Taking care of what we have: participatory natural resource management on the Caribbean coast of Nicaragua* (editor and co-author, 2000), *Para una mina de oro se necesita una mina de plata: historiando sobre la Costa Caribe de Nicaragua 1910 – 1979* (2000), and *Connected: insights from the 2nd international Community-Based Natural Resource Management workshop* (2001).